BEYOND
THE
REVOLUTION

Also by Ray Mungo

Famous Long Ago
Total Loss Farm
Between Two Moons
Tropical Detective Story
Return to Sender
Cosmic Profit
Confessions from Left Field
Lit Biz 101

BEYOND THE REVOLUTION

My Life and Times Since Famous Long Ago

RAY MUNGO

CB

CONTEMPORARY
BOOKS

CHICAGO

Library of Congress Cataloging-in-Publication Data

Mungo, Ray. 1946-
   Beyond the revolution : my life and times since Famous long
ago / Ray Mungo.
       p.   cm.
   ISBN 0-8092-4260-5
     1. Mungo, Raymond, 1946-   2. Intellectuals—United
States—Biography.   3. Authors, American—20th century—
Biography.   4. Baby boom generation—United
States.   I. Title.
CT275.M755A3   1990
070′.92—dc20   90-1800
   [B]   CIP

"The Road Not Taken" from *The Poetry of Robert Frost* edited by
Edward Connery Lathem, © 1916, © 1969 by Holt, Rinehart and
Winston, © 1944 by Robert Frost reprinted by permission of Henry
Holt and Company, Inc.

Material from "Sabotaging the Dissident Press" by Angus Mackenzie
from *Columbia Journalism Review* reprinted by permission.

Material from *Creative States Quarterly* reprinted by permission.

"Sonnet on Kurt's Sixtieth" by John Updike reprinted by permission.

"A Prosody" by Norma Farber reprinted by permission.

Material from "What Is a Writer?" by Claire Braz-Valentine reprinted
by permission.

Material from Steve d'Arazien's letter of June 10, 1989, reprinted by
permission.

Material from "These States" by Allen Ginsberg reprinted by
permission.

"God help us refugees in winter dress" by Verandah Porche
reprinted by permission.

Published by Contemporary Books, Inc.
180 North Michigan Avenue, Chicago, Illinois 60601
Manufactured in the United States of America
International Standard Book Number: 0-8092-4260-5

For Robear

Contents

Acknowledgments

No BOOK IS A SOLITARY EFFORT, however lonesome this business of writing may be. Many people helped create this book, principal among whom were Jane Dystel, agent extraordinaire; editors Nick Bakalar, Nancy Coffey, Karin Horgan, and Ann Peters at Contemporary Books; Verandah Porche and Richard Wizansky at Total Loss Farm; authors Angus Mackenzie, Sydney Omarr, Jessica Mitford, Tom Robbins, Norma Farber, John Updike, Armistead Maupin, Claire Braz-Valentine, and George Warren; Nancy Mayer of Carmel and New York; John Wilton and Steve Diamond, veteran stalwarts of Liberation News Service and the Fellowship of Religious Youth; Writers' Jamboree conspirators Michael Golden, George Fuller, Al Goodman, Shayna Selby, Ellen Weiner, Farouk Shield, Frank Stark, M.D., Michael E. Clark, Paco Soares, Carolyn Higashi, Jessica Everingham, and Anne Holliday; Cynthia Williams, Yolanda Shea, and Ephraim and Rosa Doner of Carmel Highlands.

BEYOND
THE
REVOLUTION

The Road Not Taken

Two roads diverged in a yellow wood,
And sorry I could not travel both
And be one traveler, long I stood
And looked down one as far as I could
To where it bent in the undergrowth;

Then took the other, as just as fair,
And having perhaps the better claim,
Because it was grassy and wanted wear;
Though as for that the passing there
Had worn them really about the same,

And both that morning equally lay
In leaves no step had trodden black.
Oh, I kept the first for another day!
Yet knowing how way leads on to way,
I doubted if I should ever come back.

I shall be telling this with a sigh
Somewhere ages and ages hence:
Two roads diverged in a wood, and I—
I took the one less traveled by,
And that has made all the difference.

—Robert Frost

BOOK I
FAMOUS LONG AGO AGAIN

Chapter 0
Memere, Liberace, and Me

OF ALL THE OLD STORIES swapped and relived at my father's three-day wake, none was more enjoyable than that of my grandmother's affair with Liberace. Marie LaFontaine was my mother's mother, had twenty kids by the same profligate Quebecois husband and a life as hard and rocky as the soil of Trois Rivières, where she was born. She spoke no English supposedly, but I once heard her break into it with a passion when a grocer tried to slip her an overripe tomato. "My money good!" she shrieked, waving a silver certificate valued by the U.S. government at one dollar in precious metal. "Why you giving me bad *tamate?*"

The grocer quickly replaced it with a firmer version. "Memere, you spoke English!" I said. "*Non!*" She didn't want to give up her familiar patois.

Anyway, Memere first saw television in 1952, when she was seventy-five and I was six years old, and she believed the people on TV were really and truly in our living room and could see and hear her as well as she could see them. No amount of argument could convince her otherwise, so we let her indulge in this apparently harmless delusion. I'm far

3

from sure, however, that this early conditioning isn't responsible for my lifelong affinity with the medium. I can suspend my disbelief with a readiness that borders on being terrifying, but Memere related to the characters on TV as guests in our home.

Her personal favorite was Liberace. He flashed those pearly teeth especially for her, tickled those eighty-eights to tickle her heart in the process. And she utterly refused to watch him until she put on her best dress, lipstick, rouge, earrings, talcum powder, perfume, nylon stockings, Sunday shoes, and a pearl necklace and of course put in her teeth. Thus dolled up, she would take her place on the sofa in front of the old Sylvania console and wait with unconcealable excitement for Liberace to visit her again.

In the '50s nobody accused Liberace of being gay. Memere didn't live to see him sued for palimony by a blond boyo. She was madly in love with the guy and cooed, waved, blew kisses at him, and called him her boyfriend, *cher tresor*, little cabbage. Sunday afternoons at our tenement revolved around getting her ready for Liberace, and soon the whole neighborhood began dropping by to see the lady who believed TV was real.

My Aunt Antoinette, one of my mother's many sisters, came down from Lewiston, Maine, to our place in Lawrence, Massachusetts, determined to convince Memere of her foolishness. She spread out family photographs on the kitchen table, patiently explaining that while we could see Uncle Rene and Aunt Betty in the snapshot, *they* couldn't see us. Memere nodded in agreement; so far, so good. She turned on the TV and issued a whole volley of French swear words at Kukla, Fran, and Ollie. ("*Eh, maudit!*") "You see, Ma, dey don' hear me talking like dose words, dey just keep playing." Memere agreed again but with a mournful look of skepticism; I suspect she thought Kukla, Fran, and Ollie didn't understand French cursing. Like a trial lawyer building to a summation, my aunt swooped in with the triumphant logical conclusion: "Ma, Liberace can't see you!"

Memere nodded solemnly, got up, and started getting

dressed. Liberace would be on in an hour, barely enough time to get ready. We were doubled over with laughter as an apoplectic Antoinette plotted her coup de grace. Memere finally entered the living room, dressed to the teeth and beaming with joy. Liberace came on and went into his first number after introducing his mother and brother George. My aunt backed up to the TV, raised her skirt, and lowered her panties, throwing a moon at Liberace. Pandemonium broke out in the room, with my grandmother screaming at my aunt for showing her ass to Liberace, my aunt screaming that he didn't see it, and the rest of us howling and gasping for air.

The following Sunday, the Suez Canal crisis was upon us, and boring old Eisenhower took over all three networks. Liberace wasn't on, and Memere was a brokenhearted lover jilted on prom night, left at the altar. "Of course he didn't come back to this house," she lamented, "after my daughter showed him her ass last week."

Although very young at the time, I knew Memere was going to die the day she was too sick to entertain Liberace. She wouldn't let him see her in a bathrobe, old and dying, but I wheeled her into the kitchen where she could steal peeks at him through the living room door without being seen. She died in the night, that kind of anticipated death that is both a grief and a relief to the survivors, and brought on a rollicking three-day wake with cousins by the dozens and sleepin' at the foot of the bed. The only difficulty was that our parents strictly forbade us to turn on the TV during the mourning period—which, even at the time, seemed ironic. Memere wouldn't have missed an episode of "The Cisco Kid" out of respect for the faithfully departed.

(Each episode ended with Cisco and Pancho riding off shouting "Good-bye, amigo, see you soon, hahahahaha-haha!" Memere waved enthusiastically, returning the "Good-bye, amigo" line, certainly the only Spanish word she ever knew. But when Cisco was facing mortal danger, say bad guys in a shoot-out, she gripped the side of the chair with white-knuckled fingers or hid her face in pure terror.)

While our great concern was missing the antics of Howdy Doody and his pals, days and nights were spent in the purple gloom of Racicot's Funeral Home, where Memere lay dressed for Liberace but looking grayer and deader every day. We children watched the ritual with awe-stricken incomprehension; what does a child know of death beyond the dazzle of candlelight, sounds of muffled weeping and sad, wailing organ chords, smell of a thousand flowers, and a wake table laden with pâtés and croissants? Late May and early June had dispelled the New England winter and cold spring, and the earth we laid Memere in seemed warm, loamy, safe harbor for a peasant and good *tamate*.

The Lawrence, Massachusetts, of thirty years ago hasn't changed. The place looks the same—grim, mile-long red-brick mills; "three-decker" houses teeming with kids and grandparents; and the great Merrimack River slashing over the grand falls and powering the factories. Catholic churches define ethnic neighborhoods that have been ravaged by desertions; Puerto Ricans, Haitians, Vietnamese cram families into apartments that once held Irish, French-Canadian, Polish, and Italian people who came to Lawrence a generation earlier for the same reasons, for the minimum-wage sweatshop labor and cheap flats. But the old settlers now defile the new ones with racist slurs, gun battles and race riots erupt in the streets, murder and burglary are common, and Lawrence has been rated by the Rand McNally *Places Rated Almanac* as the least desirable area in which to live in the United States.

Tell it to the old bucks at the LaSalle Social Club on Andover Street, where my Uncle Roland presided over the card table and threw a wild wedding for his junior. When I was impatient for something, my mother'd say, "Rome wasn't built in a day," which as a small kid I heard as "*Roland* wasn't built in a day." So I imagined my uncle being built, step by step, over several days.

Lawrence is Jack Kerouac territory, although he lived downriver in Lowell and beat us in the annual Thanksgiving

Day high school football game. Nobody from Lowell would want to be associated with Lawrence and vice versa, although to an outsider they appear startlingly alike, sisters in the ethic of toil.

My father worked for thirty years for a paper mill and loved it. Great rolls of pulp newsprint were spun like cotton candy out of vats of wet, smelly gray matter; when the giant turbines switched on, the clatter and bellow of the machinery was deafening, terrifying to a small child but sweet music to my old man. He knew all the boys in the pressing and dyeing rooms, the ones who hot-rodded around on forklifts, who took delivery from rusty freight cars on the platform, who dried and packaged the fresh rolls, who drove the trucks loaded with pulp to newspaper plants in Concord, New Hampshire, and Pawtucket, Rhode Island. The boys' names were my father's nightly suppertime litany; we heard, over and again, what Vinnie Manion said to Charlie Larkin on the second shift (that Vinnie is a hot shit) and what's new with Al Gross, Dr. Van Nostrand, Jim Beaulieu, Joe Malone, and Gil St. Pierre—a great bunch of guys, a crew of playmates in a man's world insulated forever against the influence of the female persuasion.

Here at Merrimack Paper, we're very, very merry Mac! At fourteen, I'd decided it symbolized everything about Lawrence that made me obsessed with a personal crusade to get out. It was the very "dark Satanic mill" that Blake wrote about, that hung a dark cloud over my (intended) future as chief drama critic of the *New York Times*—but not of course until after a lengthy apprenticeship under Brooks Atkinson *and* the successful production of my first dozen plays. But for my dad, Merrimack Paper was home away from home, a men's consciousness group before such pretenses were devised.

His other great love was the Catholic church, specifically St. Patrick's, in the shadow of whose towering spires my father would live his entire life. St. Pat's parish naturally catered to the spiritual needs of the Irish, who also controlled the political machine in town, so the parish was

relatively better endowed, the church relatively grander, than
the smaller churches serving Wops, Polacks, and Frogs. My
father's mother, Nana, came from County Cork, so we
qualified as Irish despite his father being a Scottish Presby-
terian. I never met my grandfather, but he spent the last
twenty years of his life in the state-operated insane asylum in
Danvers, a true pit of despair and acrid odors along the lines
of mother England. The place lurked behind gray fieldstone
walls covered with a hundred years' accumulation of moss
and pigeon shit. The bus that took me from Lawrence to
prep school in Danvers stopped there every morning; a
withered old lady in a bathrobe got on every day to ask all
the high school boys if we'd seen her missing son.

Dad had wanted to become a religious brother and
spent several of his teenage years in seminary at Poughkeepsie, New York. He kept a letter from Brother Superior attest-
ing that he was honorably dismissed due to a nervous condition that prohibited him from public speaking, but he lived
in a reverie of those days and no doubt hoped one of his sons
would don the cloth. The brothers, he liked to say, were
"real men." Merrimack Paper became his new sanctuary
chapel.

The priests nearly snared me in the eighth grade. A
certain father notoriously and openly seduced the boys,
myself included, and got away with it for years because, I
suppose, he had mastered the art of catering to boys' lusts of
all kinds. He showered his favorites with trips to the ocean,
authorized absences from school, ice cream, beer, outings of
all sorts that always ended in a dark, locked room. Thus
already admitted to the sacred fraternity, I was chosen to
spend a week in a boys' seminary, a retreat from the world
and an introduction to the arcane secret society of pubescent
confessors. Although not convinced of the wisdom of being
shanghaied away from childhood, liberty, siblings, and
friends, I was willing to accede to the pressures from Holy
Mother Church and sign myself in with my father's proud
blessings, until my real mother put her foot down.

In so doing, she also put the carrots down, hard, on the

supper table. "This boy," she said, pointing at my nose, "doesn't know anything about women. When he's old enough to know about women, he can decide for himself if he wants to be a priest! And that's the end of it!" We waited for the inevitable explosion of my father's youthful temper, but none came. The matter was never again discussed.

A father feels a responsibility to give his son some inspiration, some example, of how to be a man, of how to be in general. Sons in turn delight in flaunting their independence of the old man's philosophy, but the influence remains. Much of the tension and unspoken distance between my father and me disappeared when I presented him with a grandson and myself became the old man, wildly different in style perhaps, but no less difficult.

When angry, my father could shake the foundations of the house with his stentorian roar. His was the justice of the almighty stark fist of removal, but no punishment was worse than the family rosary hour, on your knees on the cold oilcloth kitchen floor. As he got older, his anger subsided, finally disappearing altogether as he slipped into an incurable, infinite depression. He was spared the indignities of the state nuthouse, but the expensive, locked confines of the psycho ward of a pious Catholic hospital was little better.

St. Dymphna's ward, brilliant with chrome and neon lighting, rotten with castaways drooling or ranting at no one in particular, was the loony bin of my nightmares; and my father in it was crying softly in a corner, just so down there was no sense or point in living anymore. Electric shock treatments to his poor brain left him staring into space, unable to read the three-day-old *Lawrence Eagle Tribune* he held in his hands, miserable and lost. Is this it? Retirement? What am I supposed to do when there's nothing to do? We sat with him those gloomy hours, fending off attack from the demented, but my father was never crazy, just drained of purpose and hope and fearing the other side, the chasm between here and over there. He prayed more fiercely than ever, alone on his knees now, clutching tattered prayer cards from the seminary of his long ago; he prayed, I imagine, for deliverance from the dark horror chambers of his mind, the ones that made him cry out in the night and eat the mood pills that reduced him to a zombie.

He died on the morning that he was to reenter the hospital, on the anniversary of his mother's death, on the kind of January morning in Massachusetts that threatens survival itself with the icy grip of brutal cold. The land was locked in ice, clouds hovered blackly over St. Patrick's old arches, and the wind slashed down from Canada and Maine, an unforgiving, knifing pain. The call came at 8 A.M. Pacific time in a small beach cottage in California, a golden state that in my childhood dreams had been a fantasy too extravagant to resist. A place where it's always summer, where January doesn't bite and Walt Disney in his eternal generosity beckons us to play! And the California of my adult life is not disappointing in any of those respects.

"Daddy's dead." It was my beatnik brother, who operates a combination art cinema–legitimate theater–poetry center in the charming neo-Colonial former whaling village of Newburyport. "He just got out of bed and keeled over with a heart attack. Ma's here, I'll put her on. You got enough money to fly home?"

I packed six sweaters but neglected to include any underwear except for a long-forgotten pair of thermal long johns, soul companions on a trip to the faithful departed.

The family arrived early at the funeral home to view the body. The car wouldn't start in the relentless weather, and neighbors guarded the house against obituary-reading burglars. The first sight of Dad, embalmed and embanked in flowers, drove my sister's twelve-year-old daughter into fits of uncontrollable weeping; I held her, feeling in her tears a release of my own, hearing myself saying all those clichéd assurances: "He's in a better place now." "He has no pain now, he's at peace, he's sleeping, we'll meet him again in heaven." What does a child know of death beyond the dazzle, sounds, and smells?

The relatives, friends, coworkers, and church associates arrived in waves. The story, often retold, of Memere's affair with Liberace was only one of what seemed hundreds of old tales that, together with copious amounts of liquor, eased our transition, our adjustment to the reality that he's gone and withdrew, am I blue? Was I gay? Am I blue? The voice of Billie Holiday crowded my mind, superimposed over the funereal strains of Latin hymns, murmuring of prayers, endless choruses of "Sorry for your trouble."

My best friend from childhood, a virtual brother in the commission of many small sins (including the time we pushed an abandoned car into the Merrimack River and sniggered in delight as it went over the falls), returned to me from many years of estrangement. George and I parted ways over the Vietnam War, he to Saigon and an environment as close to hell on earth as he'll ever survive and I to the picket lines, protest marches, and frenetic organizing of the antiwar, underground press. Time ultimately convinced him that people like me were not really evil anti-American Communists and the war not really a noble cause. Especially galling, of course, was the tepid and even hostile reception he got on returning home, no hero but an unfortunate who had neither the resources to go to college nor the chicanery to outwit the draft. Especially comforting was the realization that we hadn't changed, that we were still at heart good bad boys in our crude treehouse, devoted to harassing our older sisters, stealing gum from Luke the Belgian grocer (who sat in his back room transfixed by the McCarthy hearings on TV and boasted that he had never seen a banana before coming to the United States, the greatest country on earth), and sneaking peeks at a neighbor man's *Playboy* magazines. (The neighbor was the only Protestant on the block and had a retarded son we sometimes babysat. I remember thinking at the time that only Protestants were allowed to read *Playboy*, and about Jews, who knew? There simply weren't any.)

"Good morning heartache, here we go again." Old Billie wouldn't leave me at a time like this. The morning of the funeral dawned freezing and overcast. We carried my father up the icy steps of St. Pat's and heard the old thunder-and-lightning priest deliver his booming eulogy: "Rejoice because he is with his God, rejoice because he is happy in heaven!" Do I believe it? Am I blue? The cemetery was as I remembered it, the plot having long ago been set aside for us, but the Commonwealth of Massachusetts in its eminent domain had constructed an eight-lane highway through it, so my father lies in earshot of hell-for-leather diesel trucks and rushing commuters en route to Boston. We stood on ice sheets and heard the final prayers and laid him in earth so cold it had to be blasted open. Now he, and we, wait for spring, while I cheat the elements by keeping what's left of my sanity in a warmer climate.

I don't know where we go when we die, if we can be said to exist at all. Perhaps there is some posthumous couch in the sky where Memere, Liberace and his blond boyo, my father, and I can enjoy all-eternity viewing. Lawrence Welk will play champagne music for my father, June Cleaver will serve angel-food cake, Jack Paar will weep, and Uncle Mil-tie'll come in drag. Pass the ambrosia and popcorn.

I lived and I will die with these people. Famous or otherwise, long ago or now.

Chapter 1
Who Put the Bomp in the Bomp Shi Bomp Shi Bomp?

BUT WHO OR WHAT really killed Marshall Bloom? He died November 1, 1969, after my first book, *Famous Long Ago: My Life and Hard Times with Liberation News Service*, was written but not yet published. Marshall had read the manuscript and predicted the book would be a huge success, which proved true. Robert Redford, then the Sundance Kid, promptly bagged film rights.

Liberation News Service, or LNS, was our underground press news agency, a kind of AP or UPI for the antiwar and hippie elements. Marshall and I were the original founders with a woman named Bala-Bala, who has since gone underground.

Bloom's death was ruled a suicide. He was found in his car, a hose running from the tailpipe into a wing window, snuffed by carbon monoxide while reading the *New York Times*. That same newspaper later printed an op-ed page commentary by David Eisenhower, then son-in-law to the president of the United States, essentially using Marshall's demise as symbolic of "the decline of the counterculture."

The dedication to the book, hastily added just as it was

going to press in late 1969, reads: "This is dedicated to Marshall Irving Bloom (1944–1969), who was too good to be also wise. Some months after I completed this manuscript, Marshall went to the mountain-top and, saying, 'Now I will end the whole world,' left us confused and angry, lonely and possessed, inspired and moved but generally broken."

But there is much more here than meets the eye. Scholar Angus Mackenzie revealed in the *Columbia Journalism Review* in the early 1980s that LNS had been thoroughly infiltrated by paid FBI informers posing as radical journalists. Mackenzie gained access to previously sealed records via the Freedom of Information Act. We know that Bloom in particular was targeted as the most "dangerous" of our band of true radicals and that he was threatened with public exposure of his alleged homosexuality by anonymous callers and letters—almost certainly the work of the FBI, which specialized in poison-pen documents attacking LNS and Bloom.

We know the government set fire to our Washington, D.C., office building in the middle of the night, while we slept in it. We have every reason to suspect that paid agents hounded Bloom to his death, because Marshall was deathly afraid of being called gay. He was, in fact, a gay celibate, someone with the inclination but no lover. He kept body-building magazines with photos of young male models in briefs, the closest thing to gay pornography that 1969 offered; they were stolen from under his bed by dissident LNS staff (actually FBI infiltrators) who threatened to use them as evidence against him.

That same year, the famous Stonewall Rebellion in New York City gave birth to the gay liberation movement, which was to prosper in the licentious 1970s. Meanwhile, Bloom's closeted friends, shaken by his suicide, came out.

I was one of those, and I lost my mind along with my inhibitions. With royalties from *Famous Long Ago* and my second book, *Total Loss Farm*, which was also successful, I embarked on a life of more or less constant pleasure-seeking.

Work was anathema, and I was determined never to have a job in my life. By living communally with a dozen or more friends on a hundred-acre farm deep in the backwoods of Vermont, I was able to get by without compromising the ideals we had saved from the antiwar movement.

We lived on brown rice, LSD, mescaline, group sex, Eastern religion, homegrown pot, Vermont maple syrup, Volkswagen bugs and buses, and "youth fare," half-price airline tickets offered to people under twenty-five on a stand-by basis. I ran around Europe, Central America, South America, Asia, and all forty-eight continental states of the Union plus Hawaii in a demented pursuit of love and adventure, gathering material for the five books that followed *Total Loss Farm* and hundreds of articles and stories published in journals as respectable as *The Atlantic*, as raunchy as *Playgirl*, as radical as *Mother Jones*.

Tropical Detective Story, my only novel, details the insanity of the first few years after Bloom's death, when I came out of the closet but fell hopelessly in love with one straight guy after another, setting myself up for the pain of unrequited affection and international flight. Chapter twenty-three opened: "The road is rough as nails but it has its compensations. The homeless pay no gas or electric bills and needn't adjust their lovely strangenesses under any subtle community pressures. When the vibes cool off, just split. . . . Alone is homeless; homeless is Alone."

Jake Dobson in this story was Steve Diamond, mentioned in *Famous Long Ago* as the mastermind who staged the U.S. premier of the Beatles' film *Magical Mystery Tour* as a benefit for LNS and used the money to help Bloom purchase the LNS farm in Montague, Massachusetts. Trespassers Will was Paul Williams, the founder of *Crawdaddy* magazine and author of a number of books including *Das Energi*. Eustacia Vye was poet Verandah Porche, another mainstay of LNS and Total Loss Farm, and even Robert Redford got in there as Ben Redwing, the Sundown Kid. I passed myself off as Dennis Lunar because "Dennis is only 'sinned' spelled backwards, and Lunar means Moon-go."

Dennis's philosophy: "Lonely California Pisces dude seeks self-destruction at the hands of God, seeks the Garden of Eden factory rebuilt, seeks an honorable end to all this pain. Lonely California Pisces dude reminds me of Rimbaud. Who will smoke a joint with me (the reefer as big as the Ritz) and forget it?"

As the novel comes to an end, Dennis/Raymond is boarding a freighter ship in Powell River, British Columbia, bound for Kobe, Japan. That trip took me all over Japan, Hong Kong, Thailand, Malaysia, Indonesia, India, and Nepal and was the basis of my book *Return to Sender*, a kind of stoned odyssey to the Orient, Siddhartha on psychedelics. I left with no return ticket, lost my heart in Tokyo and all my money in Calcutta, and spent months wandering around in a loincloth searching for my guru, who turned out to be an old ganja-smoking hermit on the mountain path between Kathmandu and Tibet.

"In this life," he said, "you are either a householder or a monk. And *you* are not a monk. Now go home and have children."

Children? It hardly seemed possible for a gay guy with a major hang-up on young Japanese men—oh, those nights in Shinjuku!—but after my second go-around in Japan, and after a Kyoto friend got busted with Thai marijuana I'd given him, I left Japan in a blaze of paranoia and found myself in New York City fathering a son with an eccentric astrologer woman who had been foretold of my coming by a psychic. Or so she said. She was still legally married to the father of her two-year-old daughter, so we left the country (she told customs officials that her husband was dead) and carried the pregnancy through the jungles of Costa Rica and Nicaragua until health problems forced us back to the U.S. The kid was born in a small clinic north of Seattle.

The Pacific Northwest provided a safe environment in which to be crazy, so we bought a house and opened a literary bookstore and small press publishing operation, Montana Books, but I continued to run around the country on limited funds, in old cars, on Amtrak sleepers and red-eye cheap flights, gathering experiences and anecdotes for new books *Cosmic Profit*, *How to Make Money Without Doing Time* (a study of hip young entrepreneurs), and *Confessions from Left Field: A Baseball Pilgrimage* (possibly the strangest baseball book ever written). And I continued to be gay.

In 1978 I left Seattle postdivorce, carrying only what would fit in the car, and retraced my steps to the small-town neighborhood of Carmel, California, where I'd rented a cabin and written *Tropical Detective Story* years earlier. Here I was absorbed into a community of like-minded citizens, rich ex-Communists with Hollywood blacklist credentials and burned-out former '60s radicals, but the gay subculture was virtually nonexistent and I'd decided to move back to New York in 1981 when by some miracle I met the man of my dreams in a Carmel sushi bar.

He combined delightful elements of being ethnically pure Japanese but culturally pure Hollywood born and raised. We moved to L.A. and promptly sublet the home of *Midnight Cowboy* author James Leo Herlihy. After six months and many harrowing misadventures in the screen trade, we fled to the village of Haiku, Maui, where we became jungle bunnies living off the proceeds of the dope harvest (eight dollars an hour and all you could smoke for clipping the bud from the stalks and packaging the stuff for shipping to da mainland), the fruit from da trees, and pineapples from da fields. No editor in New York sent a check to any writer living in Haiku, Maui. Weeeeell, the one exception might have been our neighbor, poet W. S. Merwin, but who knows how poets make a living? Alicia Bay Laurel, the bestselling author of *Living on the Earth*, supports herself on Maui as a pop singer.

Eventually of course we came back to California, and Palm Springs is now home base for further wanderings and ponderings.

Now, dear reader, you know enough about me to get the general picture. The one thing all those previous books, starting with *Famous Long Ago*, had in common was that they chronicled the lives of my generation, the baby boomers if you will, the people for whom the 1960s and '70s were a period of youth and growth, the 1980s a time to turn forty or nearly, the 1990s a time to assume mature leadership, and the year 2000 our date with fate. The new millennium will test our character.

This book aims to bring us up to date on what tran- spired between then and now with all those zany characters from the original hip soap opera and tell where we're going next and why. Some of us remained in the public eye: Tom Hayden married Jane Fonda, which certainly guaranteed continued celebrity, even when they separated; Abbie Hoff- man emerged from a period of hiding underground to evolve into a stand-up comedian with a conscience, though he died depressed; Jerry Rubin has not lost his touch for grabbing media attention. Others of us retreated into a more private world, even going straight, so to speak, or returning to ancestral religions. We'd like to find those people too, find how they are readying for the millennial revolution.

So get ready. If you have children, as many of us do, you may be even more concerned for the future of the world— although properly speaking we are *all* related as brothers and sisters, parents and kids, under one sky on one very endangered planet. Acid rain, AIDS, crack cocaine, green- house effect, ozone holes, Star Wars, nuclear meltdowns are just a few of the new threats that leave you feeling the decade of the '60s, for all its hellish war in Vietnam, was child's play. Now we're up against the Creeping Meatball, *whoa*. Can't sit down, gotta save the world, after all these past twenty years and everything we've done, things seem to have gotten *worse*.

Talk about *Living on the Earth*, where is Alicia Bay Laurel now that we need her? What ever happened to the divinely crazed Warren Hinckle, founder of *Ramparts* mag- azine? What's new with Mark Rudd, James Simon Kunen, Arlo Guthrie, Joni Mitchell, Eldridge Cleaver, Joan Baez, Jesse Kornbluth, Barbara Garson, Timothy Leary, Mildred Loomis, Steve Lerner, Jessica (*American Way of Death*) Mitford, Charles (*Greening of America*) Reich, and Harvey

"Sluggo" Wasserman, hmmm? If you recognize half or more of these names, go to the head of the class, but even if you don't, you're welcome to get on the bus and trip out. . . .

What follows is a story, by no means complete, of what happened to us and how we survived through the 1980s—at least for those who *did*. I hope you enjoy it as I have, at least much of the time, enjoyed putting it down for you. Please don't try to find some kind of exotic message in all this; it's life and life only and thank goodness it's still worth living and even laughing over. OK, here goes nothin'. . . .

Chapter 2
Liberation News Service, the Seedy Presence Revealed

WASHINGTON, D.C., LAND of the free, homeless, and brave, was where we started Liberation News Service, not of choice but necessity. The year was 1967, and Marshall Bloom and I were recent college graduates who had edited our respective campus newspapers (Amherst College and Boston University) and were hired by the U.S. Student Press Association in Washington to one-year terms as directors. USSPA, like the National Student Association, which spawned it, was a lobbying outfit and membership association representing college newspapers.

Bloom and I were members of the dissident counterculture, whatever you want to call it, young guys opposed to the war in Vietnam who burned our draft cards in protest, smoked pot and cigarettes and anything else we could get our hands on, grew long hair, and wanted to *do something* in support of the new crop of "underground" newspapers. We decided to use USSPA's comfortable treasury and offices to lure this emerging media into collaboration with the college press.

The underground press of the time was not literally under the earth, but almost so. Typically these papers were

20

issued weekly, monthly, or whenever a ragtag staff could get it together, then sold on the street by whoever was poor enough to do so. The ethic of this antiwar generation prohibited "work" in the sense of a regular job, so these papers supported people who were on the fringe of society, mostly middle-class children disillusioned with the government, schools, "straight" society, etc. They printed swear words and nude photographs, both enticing and horrifying to polite society at the time.

(It seems incredible twenty years later, when we're accustomed to "adult bookstores" and explicit pornography quite within the law, but in 1967 Boston's *AVATAR* newspaper was seized by police under obscenity laws for printing a commonly known four-letter word.)

In short, there was *no way* the U.S. Student Press Association membership, which included some highly conservative schools like West Point, wanted to be associated with the underground press or for that matter with Bloom, who'd been elected sight-unseen by mail ballot. And when the assembled mostly shorthaired, white male college editors of the land got a load of Marshall at the group's annual convention in Minneapolis that year, they fired him on the spot.

He was outrageous and couldn't hide it. Impossibly skinny and crowned with a Harpo Marx curly mop, he wore granny glasses, spoke nonstop in a breathless tumble of words and ideas, brooked no opposition, and flaunted his radical beliefs with a megalomaniacal self-confidence that drove his enemies crazy. Steve Lerner, writing in the *Village Voice*, described Marshall as "a gaunt young man of insufferable allergies." He slept about four hours a night and zoomed around in a tiny green Triumph sports car, faithfully attended by his equally hyper Irish setter, Max.

His friends just had to put up with Marshall the way he was; we wouldn't have tried to change him. He was difficult, but he was usually right and his talents were amazing.

Although he looked like a freak from the nearest opium den, Bloom could, for example, get credit at the bank, manipulate a distributor of paper and office supplies, convince a hotel clerk that he was the manager of a rock group (and

skip out in the morning without paying the room bill), or
talk a landlord into a lease. But when he published a volatile
pamphlet and distributed it under the USSPA name, the
editors voted to oust him, grateful for an official reason.
Actually they just couldn't stand his *personality*.

I was more tolerable an employee, but I shared Marshall's beliefs and convictions about the issues of the day and
so promptly resigned my USSPA job in sympathetic protest
of the vote. It was as much an act of personal loyalty and
friendship as politics. In any case, the prospect of working
for those uncool college editors lacked much appeal.

The office secretary, Barbara "Bala-Bala" Heimlich,
joined us in the protest; we three brave ones stood to the
side and exhorted the few editors still with us to rally behind
a new, independent news service. LNS was born, broke and
owing.

We went straight back to Washington and ripped off
USSPA's office supplies on behalf of LNS, the movement,
and peace on earth. Ours became an outlaw existence, and
Bloom was the foxiest of the lot. Abbie Hoffman, author of
Steal This Book, called him "the most clever thief I've ever
known." But Marshall was profoundly honest in a personal
sense and sincerely believed in the morality of our cause.

We could have opened shop anywhere except for the fact
that the USSPA jobs had led us to lease a brownstone house
on Church Street near the office and Dupont Circle, and we
were stuck in Washington, D.C., lacking funds to move.
Considering that we managed to trash the house completely
in a year's time, after filling it with transients, drugs, printing presses, and so forth, it's ironic that we actually felt a
moral obligation to the twelve-month lease.

The lady who owned the house had been *so* nice. A
Virginia gentlewoman, she was taken by Marshall's high-
toned speech about his job as executive director of the
association (my title was international news director) and his
background at the London School of Economics. What he
didn't tell her was that he led the first student uprising in
centuries at LSE, triggering a fatal heart attack in an elderly

porter, and that the tabloid *Boston Record American* once
ran an editorial suggestion that I be deported to Cuba.

We expected to share the place as residential bachelors
when we rented it, but within weeks the house had become
office, crash pad, and mailing center of LNS and the organizational nerve center of a planned demonstration at the
Pentagon. Our boarders included a teenage runaway from
New Jersey, a welfare grandmother escaped from St. Elizabeth's mental hospital, a guy who called himself General
Hershey Bar (a takeoff on General Hershey, head of the
military draft during Vietnam) and went around dressed in
a uniform saluting everybody, transient young writers, pho-
tographers, and rock musicians.

From the first, the news service was a hit. The number
of underground papers was growing fast, and an increasing
percentage of the college press subscribed as young people's
consciousness evolved and antiwar sentiment grew. We
charged fifteen dollars a month but kept mailing the stuff
whether the freak sheets paid all, some, or none of the bill.
We got our news in the mail and over the phones, typed the
stories on film sheets, mimeographed them onto brightly
colored paper on an ancient machine kept in the basement,
and sat around the living room collating, folding, address-
ing, and mailing our little homemade packets.

The thing grew beyond our ability to keep up with it.
The mimeo machine was retired in favor of an offset press
Marshall somehow acquired on credit. We were always at
war with the phone company over past-due bills. We
bounced checks. We lived for the moment and reveled in it,
and LNS reached literally millions of readers despite inade-
quate funding, chaotic administration, and youthful irre-
sponsibility.

That vast readership did not go unnoticed by the powers that ran the town. The federal government, led by the
chronically paranoid FBI chief J. Edgar Hoover, kept close
tabs on New Left youth groups like LNS, and he actually
considered us dangerous subversives. It's hard to imagine
today, but in those days anybody could arrive at the door and

within an hour be considered a member of the "staff" of an underground paper or news service. We were always grateful for any help, even if it happened to be a paid government agent posing as a crazed acid head.

We'll get deeper into the question of spies and counter-spies, infiltrators, and conspiracies later in the book when we interview that intense maven of the Center for Investigative Reporting, Angus Mackenzie. His research after passage of the Freedom of Information Act produced shocking evidence of foul play.

We did drugs with abandon. If the drug was an un-tested or a new kind, so much the better. There was an air of danger and imminency everywhere during the Vietnam War, as if an hour could be forever. Partly it was the draft that loomed over young men, but it was also the sense of anarchic doom fermented by all the killings—John and Bobby, Martin Luther King, Kent State . . . friends, these were times when just being *young* could get you shot. But that insecurity, that sense of impending doom, was not the only reason we turned to drugs. Fact is, they had the power to blow your mind, a proposition regarded as highly good at the time. Of course, people actually died from these excesses, and most of us today have long since turned away from psychedelics. Drugs are passé, kids.

Our first office building was at 3 Thomas Circle, a crumbling but centrally located building just blocks from the White House and big enough for LNS to share with a half-dozen related antiwar groups and the local under-ground paper, the *Washington Free Press*. All kinds of hell broke loose as the right-wing congressmen and senators harped on the "establishment of an American Cong head-quarters right in the nation's capital." We loved the atten-dant publicity of course, but we paid the price of continual police harassment and entrapment. Life became a battle-ground around LNS.

All of this chaos was in the spirit of news events of those days. College campuses began to explode with unrest and even bombings. Civil rights and pacifism turned to black power and militancy. Lyndon Johnson began to look more and more worried, his "Great Society" in turmoil. Washington in particular had a dangerously high crime rate, and life there was risky at best. Full-scale civil insurrection reduced the city to a smoldering war zone after Dr. King's assassination in April 1968. We perched in our Thomas Circle "liberated zone," watching the troops, smelling the acrid odors of burning buildings.

For some strange reason, Marshall had persuaded a naive Princeton student to lend him an ornate black hearse in which we planned to tour the country promoting LNS, and it was in that ghoulish funeral wagon that we all got busted in the middle of the riots. It was our dadaistic fun bus, but not funny anymore. I think it was that night in the D.C. jail, surrounded by very angry young black men, that I realized I wanted out of this life, out of this town, out of the *fray*. Enough was too much.

The bucolic myth had begun. Meanwhile, LNS had developed branch offices in Berkeley, New York, London, and so forth, phones and telex lines, and a huge staff of personnel who were paid in room and board or less. We had our little internecine disputes with Students for a Democratic Society (SDS) and the Yippies, led by Jerry Rubin, but basically we remained your happy-go-lucky band of callous youth out to shed the emperor of his clothes. Columbia University erupted in New York, quite a number of our New York people appeared on the scene, and the energy of the news service seemed to turn northward by the summer of '68.

When eventually the news service did move to New York City, it soon split into warring camps I dubbed the Virtuous Caucus (Bloom, myself, Bala-Bala, and all the original gang of Washington friends) and the Vulgar Marxists (mostly lately arrived New York ideological types who wanted democratic control). The newcomers also took great offense at Bloom's autocratic method of running the operation. In endless meetings they denounced Marshall as a tyrant, liar, and homosexual. In that time, and even in such rarefied "ultraradical" circles, gay was definitely not OK. Even in today's AIDS-scarred atmosphere, gays are visible, organized, and outspoken. In 1968 virtually *nobody* in the nation would publicly admit to being gay.

Things got worse and worse at LNS, until we decided to capture the thing back for our own people, and that required getting out of Manhattan, with its intense congregation of Marxists. We had the good fortune to get a Beatles movie premier, *Magical Mystery Tour*, donated as a benefit for LNS. Using receipts from the Beatles movie, we heisted the presses, office equipment, and records of LNS to a farm in western Massachusetts purchased by Bloom and Steve Diamond for the news service. The whole idea was to incorporate our bucolic myth into liberation from the ideologues and wild-eyed crazies.

The angry New Yorkers raided the farmhouse a few nights later, taking hostages and beating people up. It was one of the most terrifying nights any of us had ever experienced. We were punched, kicked, tortured, locked up, screamed at, and bloodied by a gang of thugs including people who'd never set foot in the LNS office, hired guns so to speak, wielding sticks and whips. But Bloom, ever the fighter, refused to divulge the whereabouts of the sacred offset press, and they returned to the city empty-handed.

The upshot of the whole widely published fracas was that two separate groups, each claiming to be the *real* Liberation News Service, published wildly different versions of LNS out of city and country. This was bad publicity for the peace movement in every way. It gave the impression that we were at odds with our own allies, confused and divided. (Of course, we didn't realize the "allies" included infiltrators and enemies.)

The interhippie dispute, as it was called, landed on page one and the evening network news. Schisms and little wars broke out in other New Left organizations. It was a time when everything was confused and the whole world seemed to be in a state of uprising and revolution.

Although our group was the true originator, the city

folks kept the news service going (indeed for fifteen years to follow), while the country folks eventually let the press freeze in the barn. Somehow news seemed less important once our back-to-nature movement got started. Instead of being surrounded by celebrities and famous causes and on the cutting edge of the revolution, we became pioneers of the new rural communes.

On the LNS farm, Bloom turned his manic energies to cucumbers and a new publication he called *Journal of the New Age*. We actually believed we'd *invented* the term *new age* a few months earlier in a car trip from the East Coast to California with poet Verandah Porche. She was the LNS poetry editor, holder of a sinecure without pay, and the car was one of those drive-aways we delivered to its owner on the coast only after taking a six-thousand-mile, two-week detour through New Orleans, the deep South, Texas, and the Southwest.

Anyway, our new age had something to do with communal living, utopian societies, nudity, Eastern religion, striving for a higher and nobler life, and distance from and independence of conventional lifestyles. The liberation we had tried to foist on the world became secondary to the liberation in our own lives. It was the dawning of the Age of Aquarius, as the rock song said, an imagined land resembling Big Sur, California, where we first dreamed it up.

We called it Kool Space. We figured there would be an end to racial, religious, and nationalistic strife, the future would be in galaxies beyond us and all of earth one united family. Hmmm, nice dream still, and looked at from outer space we're certainly all on the same blue ball. But Marshall won't be around to savor this state if it ever comes to pass.

Halloween of 1969 had been one of those spooky New England nights where maple trees of Vermont take on the dimensions of howling ghosts, and we stayed close to the farm's wood stove, sipping hot cider and listening to the wind. On the morning after, November 1 (All Saint's Day in the Christian ritual), Marshall was found dead in his silly green sports car with a hose running from the exhaust pipe into a window, slumped over the steering wheel, holding a copy of the *New York Times*.

Verandah became hysterical on hearing the news. Black November descended on our lives, a sadness and gloom so thick it threatened never to rise. If the very young commit suicide, if the brightest and the best give up so early in the fight, how could we hope to survive the winter?

The pain seemed to never end. Through the long winter we cried and wondered if we could have done more for him, if we could have given the love needed to survive.

While it oppressed us, his death may have also set some of us free. Life suddenly appeared terribly mortal and brief, and it became necessary to live it even more intensely and openly. It became necessary to come out of hiding and test the great world on its own terms, as we shall see when the story continues.

Chapter 3
What Went Down

"ANGUS MACKENZIE BECAME OBSESSED with the idea that there had been a secret government campaign to stamp out the antiwar and countercultural press that sprang up during the Vietnam War," wrote the editors of the *Columbia Journalism Review* in the March 1981 issue in prefacing Mackenzie's article, "Sabotaging the Dissident Press."

With a small grant from the Fund for Investigative Journalism, Mackenzie set out to dig up whatever evidence he could find from sources and documents unearthed under the Freedom of Information Act. He found "irrefutable evidence that agencies of the federal government had indeed done their best to put hundreds of publications out of business," the editors added.

When they called Angus "obsessed," they were hardly exaggerating. This wonderful man, this indescribable information junkie, is today about forty years old and working with the Center for Investigative Reporting in San Francisco. He still wears a ponytail and granny glasses, sports a rough beard, rides a motorcycle (Angus last year delivered a friend's birthday cake by Harley Davidson, a sorry puddle of collapsed chocolate mousse) or drives his beat-up pickup truck, lives on writing and grants from rich progressives, and works for the commonweal.

Nothing pisses off Angus Mackenzie more than seeing a government powerhouse like the FBI or CIA using its muscle and money to squash the First Amendment to the Constitution. And when Angus Mackenzie gets pissed off, *watch out.* This guy is the poor radical's version of Woodward and Bernstein; he stops at nothing to get to the truth of the matter and show the rascals for the liars and criminals they really are.

A few quotes from his *CJR* article.

The government's offensive against the underground press primarily involved three agencies—the CIA, the FBI, and the Army. In many cases, their activities stemmed from what they could claim were legitimate concerns. The CIA's Operation CHAOS, for example, was set up to look into the foreign connections of domestic dissidents; however, it soon exceeded its mandate and became part of the broad attack on the left and on publications that were regarded as creating a climate disruptive of the war effort. At its height, the government's offensive may have affected more than 150 of the roughly 500 underground publications that became the nerve centers of the antiwar and countercultural movements.

A telling example of this offensive was the harassment of Liberation News Service, which, when opposition to the Vietnam War was building, played a key role in keeping the disparate parts of the antiwar movement informed. By 1968, the FBI had assigned three informants to penetrate the news service, while nine other informants regularly reported on it from the outside. Their reports were forwarded to the U.S. Army's Counterintelligence Branch, where an analyst kept tabs on LNS founders Ray Mungo and Marshall Bloom, and to the Secret Service, the Internal Revenue Service, the

Navy, the Air Force, and the CIA. The FBI also attempted to discredit and break up the news service through various counterintelligence activities, such as trying to make LNS appear to be an FBI front, to create friction among staff members, and to burn down the LNS office in Washington while the staff slept upstairs. Before long, the CIA, too, joined the offensive; one of its recruits began filing reports on the movements of LNS staff members while reporting for the underground press to establish his cover as an underground journalist.

Oh, and there's more. Much more. Somebody named Sal Ferrera, who has since left the country and changed his name, worked as a prominent antiwar journalist and editor of one of Washington's underground papers, the *Quicksilver Times*, while simultaneously being paid by the CIA as an operative. Sometime between January and April 1970, he interviewed Abbie Hoffman and provided the CIA with personal information about the staff members at LNS. "Wherever there was radical activity, Ferrera seemed to be there," Mackenzie wrote. Ferrera was the only one of many who infiltrated our press organizations with the explicit goal of shutting them down and silencing their voices.

Thanks a lot, J. Edgar Hoover. I recall having my very own FBI agent in Washington in 1967; his name was Phil Mostrom. He interviewed me several times and used to sit drinking coffee at the People's Drug Store lunch counter across the street from our office building at 3 Thomas Circle, in a neighborhood marked by the duality of American life. One side of the circle had the luxurious Americana Hotel and Lyndon Johnson's church, the National City Christian Church (it rather sounded and looked like a bank), while the other had the rat-infested LNS building, former home of Soul Records, and the notorious all-night Eddie Leonard Sandwich Shop.

About the fire: I remember it well, but of course we thought it accidental at the time. The only reason we all

survived is that Marshall had taken in a fifteen-year-old
runaway youth who was sleeping in a downstairs closet,
smelled smoke, and woke us up. The very idea, however, that
my own government actually tried to *kill* me for no better
reason than being an idealistic twenty-one-year-old kid just
out of school, turning out homemade newspaper articles on
a battered mimeograph machine, is unsettling.

And that's the nature of the problem. Since I don't
possess any concrete evidence of harm inflicted on my body,
for example, I'm not able to sue the government. We can't
even name the perpetrators. However, Mackenzie's article
contains a great deal of documented evidence, and I trust his
reputation as an honest, thorough investigative reporter. In
other words, we know what went down, but we can't do a
damn thing about it. The Freedom of Information Act
doesn't really give you all the information—under the guise
of protecting national security, it declines to name names.
The "security" that supposedly protects us actually protects
them.

It's enough, indeed, to make the suspicion of foul play
in Marshall's death something more than just paranoia. We
still don't know the actual names of the FBI agents who
worked for LNS undercover—in these Freedom of Information releases, the government continues to censor out the
really incriminating stuff; the pages actually come with
large blacked-out spaces—which means that some of our
former friends were really enemies. We may never know the
true circumstances surrounding Bloom's apparent suicide.

Did they, the powers of great America, really believe
that the underground press was a clear and present danger
to the public? I have to conclude they did, as preposterous as
it seems. We had next to nothing in material resources, our
newspapers looked raggedy and amateurish for the most
part, our readers were young and, although not disenfran-
chised, hugely disillusioned with the political process. We
didn't vote. We didn't receive any money from foreign
sources—at LNS we worked for a "salary" of fifteen dollars
a week per person only when the news service could afford it,
plus room and board in communal abandon—but I suppose

if some foreigner had offered us money, we would have taken it.

We were vastly overpowered by the "straight" media, papers like the *New York Times* and *Washington Post* and major television networks that supported the Administration's position in Vietnam. The combined influence of Liberation News Service with all its subscribing papers couldn't compare to the power of even one issue of *Time* magazine, although we lived to enjoy the day that that publication printed a photo of Bloom and myself but misidentified us in the caption. I became Bloom and he was me.

(Marshall later sold Time, Inc., a subscription to LNS for three hundred dollars a month—twenty times the "underground" rate of fifteen dollars. By 1968 the giants of journalism needed LNS for background information on events at which we were the *only* reporters welcome, such as inside the student-occupied buildings during the Columbia University uprisings.)

The bad guys even created phony news services pretending to be antiwar and countercultural. "In San Francisco, the FBI set up Pacific International News Service," Mackenzie discovered. "Meanwhile on the East Coast the FBI operated New York Press Service under the direction of Louis Salzberg. NYPS offered its services to left-wing publications at attractive rates, soliciting business with a letter that read, in part: 'The next time your organization schedules a demonstration, march, picket or office party, let us know in advance. We'll cover it like a blanket and deliver a cost-free sample of our work to your office.' NYPS's cover was blown when Salzberg surfaced as a government witness in the Chicago Seven trial, during which it was disclosed that he had been an FBI informant."

"It was a lot easier for a 'news reporter' to get information than for an FBI agent," Mackenzie told me.

Salzberg and NYPS vanished but "the New York [FBI] office shrewdly turned this setback into a means of casting suspicion on Liberation News Service. The office prepared an anonymous letter, copies of which were sent to newspapers and antiwar groups, accusing LNS of being an FBI front. 'Lns (sic) is in an ideal position to infiltrate the movement at every level,' the letter stated. 'It has carefully concealed its books from all but a select few. Former employees have openly questioned its sources of operating funds. I shall write to you further on Lns for I (and several others) are taking steps to expose this fraud for what it really is—a government financed front.'

"Such, then, were the techniques used by the U.S. government to stifle freedom of expression in the late 1960s and early 1970s," Mackenzie concluded in his article.

Abbie Hoffman had the greatest one-liner on the subject of expression: "I *do* freedom of speech, other people just talk about it." Abbie was one of the original characters in *Famous Long Ago* and a mainstay of Liberation News Service, although he was never a journalist, more like a center-stage player in the drama we broadcast: The Story of Our Generation.

Oddly, Abbie was too old for us. Born in 1936, he was a good ten years ahead of the baby boom and already fifty-two at the time of his death in 1989, a well-publicized suicide. I remember thinking during the '60s that this guy was really *cool* for being over thirty and everything.

He had a terrific sense of humor, his saving grace. "Straight" radicals like Tom Hayden put forth the most boring, unreadable documents and propaganda like the "Port Huron Statement of Students for a Democratic Society (SDS)"; Abbie dealt in one-liners. He accused dour judge Julius Hoffman at the Chicago Seven conspiracy trial of being his illegitimate father.

Fellow YIPPIE (Youth International Party) founder Jerry Rubin was a ranting anarchist, even proposing the execution of major government figures like Nixon in his book *Do It!* Although a self-styled leader of the young and hip, Rubin did not attend the Woodstock festival. I know because I spent the famous Woodstock period with him in his New York City apartment, called in as one of many patch-up writers to work on his book.

But Abbie was zany, fun-loving, naturally warm and funny. After Rubin sort of went straight in the 1970s, promoting himself as a businessman and "networker," Abbie played Yippie to Jerry's yuppie in a series of public debates.

While Abbie was underground, fleeing from a cocaine bust, he remained in touch with many old friends, myself included. Around 1975–76, while I was in Seattle managing the bookstore and publishing company called Montana Books, I received a copy of a manuscript Abbie had titled *Book-of-the-Month Club Selection*. No publisher in New York would touch the book because of the title, and Abbie wouldn't change it, according to his wife, Anita. Montana Books couldn't publish it either, as we didn't have the resources or foolhardiness to go to war with the Book-of-the-Month Club.

Nothing more came from Abbie, but the book finally saw the light of day in 1980, under the new title *Soon to Be a Major Motion Picture*. It didn't make much of a stir on the literary scene, but the author's remarkable ability to live as a fictional persona while underground—Abbie became Barry Freed (what a moniker) and was publicly active in environmental protests in New York state—shows you he was clever.

He was not, however, immortal or superhuman. Not having heard from the guy in maybe fourteen years, I can't speculate on what sadness might have caused him to check out early, say good night. He seemed to be having too much fun for that, but things change, people change. The media coverage of his death was extraordinarily generous of spirit, the treatment usually accorded to show business celebrities, and maybe that's what Abbie Hoffman was. A performer. "Clown prince of the left," bubbled *People* magazine. A comedian with a purpose.

There's been too much dyin' in this book already and enough politics to last a lifetime. Like Abbie in underground hiding, we had to retreat from the world and build a new reality. We called it Total Loss Farm. Our motto was "Lose yourself."

Chapter 4
Winds of Change to Get You

I REMEMBER THE FARM the way it looked the first day we ever saw it. The two-hundred-year-old Vermont farmhouse was sadly dilapidated, in need of fresh paint and roof shingles. Through dirty, thin curtains we peered into the kitchen, with its old-fashioned wood-burning range, trademarked Home Comfort. The barn door was partway open; inside were damp bales of hay, remnants of some cow's dinner, rusted tractor parts, bits and pieces of hardware. Yellow spring sunshine shafted through holes and cracks in the roof and walls.

A sad, abandoned farm would be our new Atlantis, our paradise on earth.

We were battered veterans of the youth wars in Washington and New York. Verandah Porche wrote poetry, Peter Simon was a hip photographer just out of college, Marty Jezer was a peace worker with the Workshop in Nonviolence, Michele Clark was a counterculture journalist, Richard Wizansky was a writer and English teacher, Laurie Dodge was a New Age carpenter who later disappeared under unusual circumstances and was never seen again.

The farm was our salvation. We found it through a college friend, Don McLean, who had bought a little vacation cabin down the road a piece. It was lost on a narrow dirt road, up a glass mountain, miles from neighbors and light years from chic.

Rosie Franklin, the widow who owned the place, had taken refuge in an all-electric apartment in the town twenty miles south since the morning her husband Forrest, last of the traditional Vermont farmers, keeled over on the kitchen floor. She pointed out where he had landed.

Rosie, who has long gone to her rest, didn't care much for Forrest's relatives, and I think she wouldn't mind my saying so. She turned down the family's offer and sold the place to the hippies from the city, and that was big news in the tiny village of Guilford. The price was $25,000 for house and barn, shed and peach orchard, and ninety-four acres "more or less," according to a deed that measured the perimeters in terms of creeks and trees. The down payment was $5,000, gathered in clumps of loans from friends (Marty Jezer surrendered his life savings of $2,500, although far from sure of the wisdom of this move, and Peter Simon was most generous); the monthly mortgage of $227.10 was to be paid over ten years and was in fact paid off in 1978.

It's hard to remember the exact number of people who lived with us on the farm that first year, 1968. The core group was about a dozen in number, but friends close to us came and went. Some who migrated to us couldn't tolerate the hardships and returned to New York or Boston. Others tried to join our commune but didn't fit in and were asked to leave. As my name was one of the two on the deed, I took the proprietary authority to oust the infidels, sleeping bags and Bob Dylan records *exeunt*. Richard Wizansky and I uprooted the indoor toilet when the septic tank became hopelessly overloaded, forcing all to use the outhouse even in subzero temperatures.

Life magazine came up the mountain seeking interviews for its cover story on the new American communes. We were in the vanguard of yet another movement, actually a complex symphony of movements about the land, environment, pollution, women's rights, gay liberation, world peace, self-sufficiency, natural foods, shared resources, and psychic exploration. Despite having gone to the ends of the earth in search of peace and serenity, we were still in the news.

Our parents thought we had lost our minds completely. My mother took one look at the farm and started recalling *her* mother's stories about the hard life back on the rocky soil of Quebec, where they lacked indoor plumbing and electricity and got snowed in by the fierce winters. Why would anybody with a college education and every advantage in life regress to living on a dirt road in a backwater canyon, she wondered? Nonetheless, she pulled up in the station wagon with a portable Coleman stove and a picnic of pepper-steak sandwiches and proceeded to feed every hippie in sight.

Of course, we didn't think of the place as a hardship but as a palace beyond our dreams. The graceful meadow below our peach orchard swept to a panorama of western mountains, sunset good-bye to my Lord, come again morning. The little farmhouse stood in relief against the vast green forest, the only occupied house for miles, the nearest neighbor a dairyman down the foot of the hill. His young son turned into a fairy after flirting with our version of reality. (Clap if you believe in fairies.)

Really, we made a whole new universe out of someone else's failed attempt at agriculture. The world was quick to notice. More communes appeared on the scene, then rich tourists seeking getaway ski vacations, until finally our neighbors included John Kenneth Galbraith and Rudolph Serkin and antique dealers and rock musicians. But that all followed.

In the beginning the farm was a magic refuge from Amerika, a kingdom unto itself dubbed the Democratic Republic of Vermont, or DRV, the acronym of North Vietnam. We sincerely believed that no alien force could invade our mountaintop consciousness. Not even when the FBI

appeared on our doorstep, the agents from New York looking profoundly uncomfortable in this deeply rural setting,
did we admit to any vulnerability.

We had electricity, although it frequently broke down,
but no heat except for wood-burning stoves and an old
wood furnace, no gas range for cooking—but the breads
baked daily in Home Comfort were delicious. Telephone?
Forget it. Mail was delivered when the road was passable,
and sometimes a newspaper or two made the scene, although
at one point we actually stopped reading the news in the
sincere belief that it was bad for you. We had a television that
picked up one station from Albany, New York, but we threw
the set out the window one snowy night. "Too much of
nothing drives a man insane," as Bob Dylan sang. We did
read books, voraciously devouring each other's libraries
hauled from college daze and city schmaze. Thoreau, of
course, was a favorite. And we paid a great deal of attention
to nature.

People wondered, how do these young radicals settle
differences among themselves, do they all sleep together in
orgies, what happens when children come along, *what about
family*? But of course we thought of ourselves as "fambly,"
a nuclear unit complete with role playing (I was Grandpaw,
a kind of elder; Verandah was always our mother). We rarely
orgied, and in fact most of us were celibate. Couples got
together, split up, but the fambly remained whole and true.

Vermont winters could be brutally cold and dangerously
windswept. We were forced even further into ourselves, our
home, our karma together as brothers and sisters of the land.
Spring brought release and wild, effulgent little light of
mine, gonna let it shine. Summer was Easy Street, the
gardens bursting with reward and neighbors and tourists all
up and down the road till Labor Day scared them off. And
autumn . . . well, who's going to take on autumn in Vermont? For sheer foliage of heroics, it's unsurpassed—trees
blaze and shimmer and the frost is on the pumpkin.

The directions to this place: turn right at the old apple
tree, then straight on to morning. We borrowed the latter

phrase, as well as much of our inspiration, from James
Michael Barrie's lost boys and Peter Pan: "Of all delectable
islands, the Neverland is the snuggest and most compact;
not large and sprawly, you know, with tedious distances
between one adventure and another, but nicely crammed."

The old apple tree was just that, a landmark for generations after the long Weatherhead Hollow Pond (asked if we
could swim in it, Rosie said only, "Some do"), visible from
a distance as a beacon to the soul. The three miles straight
uphill on a narrow dirt road took us past lovely meadows
and streams, a wooden bridge crossing a rivulet, the stately
homes of summer people and an eighteenth-century graveyard, technically part of our land, with weathered stones
bearing inscriptions:

Two weeks I bore affliction sore
Physicians' skills were vain.
But in the end death came as friend
To ease me of my pain.
Death is a debt, from all 'tis due
Which I have paid and so must you.

After the graveyard came the picnic grove, where we
enacted rites of spring and gamboled naked in the summer
of our youth, then the forested road on which we gave a
right of way to Richard Wizansky's brother David and his
wife, Margot, sister of novelist Peter Gould (*Burnt Toast*),
another farm-based author. A great and final steep grade
landed at the corners, Packer's Corners, where a second dirt
road (this one partially reclaimed by forest and inhospitable
to vehicles) intersected. The farmhouse sat on the southeast
corner, the old village schoolhouse on the northeast, our
cornfield on the southwest, and the original Packer's Tavern
(now an antique dealer's fine home) on the northwest. Here,
Ethan Allen and his Green Mountain Boys gathered to
drink and carouse and fight the federals from New York.
(Vermont was, for a time, an independent nation. Some say
it still is. Anyway, sentiment against joining the Union was
widespread.)

Beyond Total Loss Farm lay only a few summer homes before the road dead-ended at the beaver pond, where we could skinny-dip in July and August, barely, in the crispy cold spring water and hoot. Beyond the end of the road, in a place only horses and people could reach, was the Baby Farm, named for the birth of a daughter named Sequoia. The farmhouse burned to the ground one night, too far for help from the volunteer firemen of town, claiming four lives. Not everything was sweetness and light in our village.

As much as we liked to believe ourselves above it, we struggled with communal politics quite a lot. The effort was to build a fair and just society, a gathering of equals, not through democracy (we never had meetings or votes) but through kindness and compassion. Nonetheless, some of us tended to lord it over the others, feelings were hurt, some people left the farm disillusioned and bitter. Most returned but not necessarily to live there. Those who stuck it out inherited the land, mortgage-free and clear, under title to our nonprofit artists' collaborative.

We had a cow named Bessie, a couple dozen chickens, one unfortunate pig, a horse who ran off and gave birth Christmas morning to a spindly legged foal. We hadn't even known she was pregnant, thought she was just getting fat. Dogs and cats had we many, those who survived the trauma of moving from city apartments, and bumblebees, goats, butterflies, deer, ducks, mosquitos, and wild coyotes of the mind.

Plants, flowers, and trees framed our universe. We had maple, pine, ash, oak, elm, peach, and apple trees and weeping willows. We grew daisies, violets, tulips, roses, potatoes, corn, onions, tomatoes, beans, and berries and made cider and maple syrup from fruit and sap, canned and sealed and preserved and froze our foodstuffs for winter.

We had magic on our side. A walk down the road was a dangerous trip to China or an excursion to the far side of consciousness under the influence of psychedelics. "It's never really the end." "Wherever you go, there you are." Simple homilies seemed like profound, earth-shaking revelations. If somebody baked a pie, it was a world-famous pie, if somebody fell in love it was *cosmic consummation celebration*. And love gone wrong, unrequited, was youthful tragedy second only to death.

I knew I'd never leave that place if I could just avoid growing up. But something more powerful than will or inclination forced me out, onto the lonesome highway and all the way around the world searching for the one thing the farm couldn't give me. Call it what you will, it was pure lust. I fell in love. It didn't work. And my unhappiness with the object of my obsession finally overwhelmed any ability to stay together, farmed out, pretending to be friends.

I hit the road to the West Coast at the end of 1971, shipped out to Japan on a container cargo freighter out of Vancouver, B.C. Before leaving the States, I'd written a letter to the farm from Salem, Oregon, on December 3:

> Some of you may experience the land as hard reality— for you it is not a "dream farm of the soul" but an actual collection of hills and trees, cows and tractors. Collecting maple sap drop by drop from trees promotes such a real-istic view, hence the laconic nature of the natives. And it's not soft country, like the steep valleys of Costa Rica, but hard and enduring land which'll clearly outlive us all. All in all, we are in danger of experiencing the land as real. But the lesson, as always, is that nothing is real, and the farm is in truth an outgrowth of fantasy-consciousness. . . . We've been given the incredible freedom to construct a whole new, imagined universe to live in. . . .
>
> Tear the planet to divots under my heels, I can never escape your love. It follows me everywhere, like my gone innocence, I carry it with me.
>
> And the new age will be an end to separation and regret.

Chapter 5
Them Old Dreams Are Only in Your Head

"IF YOU DO NOT FIND GOD in your own soul, the world will be meaningless to you." So said Kabir, an Indian poet of the Middle Ages, and if I'd really understood him in my youth I could have spared myself thousands of miles of aimless wanderings. But youth will go out and find the world, searching for the secret of the universe.

With the farm and its unhappy love affair behind me and a few thousand bucks from a publisher in my pocket, I cruised up and down the West Coast with fellow author Paul Williams until we sailed together across wild Pacific winter storms to Kobe, Japan. Those eleven days and nights locked up together in a stateroom or pacing the narrow deck in the frigid night, sucking on a cigarette, were a harrowing nightmare, and landfall in Japan came as a singular miracle. A new life.

Of course, you can never be Japanese if you're not. We tried. Paul married a rock singer named Sachiko and took her back to the States. I took to sitting zazen and studying kangi and otherwise assimilating myself, the gaijin extraordinaire in a country that fetched me as if from memory;

everything I saw produced a feeling of déjà vu. I became
convinced I'd been Japanese in an earlier lifetime. The place
seemed oddly familiar.

All Japanese cities, even in 1971, seemed like organized
riots. Things have just gotten busier and more frantic since
then; every time I return to Japan, the pace has quickened,
the buildings are taller, the people are running faster. Kobe
at midnight was still crowded and intense, with taxi head-
lights flashing off rain-slickened avenues and tiny alleyways
spilling light and jazz music onto sidewalks. Drunken busi-
nessmen staggered out of the bars, leaving curbside remind-
ers of their intemperance. It was frightening and ghoulish,
a netherworld culture of the moon. It was fiendishly attractive, a siren of the groin and soul.

What would Japan hold? The master? The man I love?

Kobe was nothing, of course, compared to Tokyo down
the line; that's the Shinkansen Line on the bullet train,
whooooosh, first class if you don't know how to order at the
ticket window.

Snowcapped Mount Fuji flew by as we ordered whiskey
and sandwiches from the tinkling carts. Stops along the line
included the gray Chicagolike sprawl of Osaka, the trem-
bling port of Yokohama on the edge of the monster, great
Tokyo where the whole of humanity converges in feverish
congress. Then the subway stops, Shibuya, Kanda, Shinjuku,
Ginza, dizzying outposts of an urban jungle stretching
farther than L.A. and quivering on the earthquake epicenter.
Sheer madness! Where would this stop, if ever? Where
would it lead? We did what anybody would do in a strange
town, what you'd do too. We started making phone calls to
strangers referred by friends.

You know what that's like in America. "Hi, Jim, my
name is Bill, and I'm a friend of Cathy's. She said to look
you up if I'm ever around Cleveland. Wanna have lunch some
time? How does your calendar look for next week?" In
Tokyo, it was more like "Excuse me very much, but I'm a
friend of Cathy's in Japan for the first time and . . . What?
Where am I? At the YMCA Kanda. You'll what? Be over here
right away? Please to wait!"

Pleased to meet you, Mamasan. Within a day we were taken under the direct sponsorship of a host family and within a week were moved out of the hotel into the crash-pad apartment of a Tokyo rock-and-roll writer and connoisseur of all things hip American. In a month I was working for Hitachi Corporation doing ads aimed at U.S. young people and writing essays for *New Music Magazine*, Tokyo gigs for street money.

Caucasian foreigners find it extremely easy to win gainful employment in Tokyo. If you're a native English speaker with a high school education you can at least teach English, at handsome rates. Black people, regardless of national origin, seem horribly discriminated against in Japan, and other kinds of Asians are generally relegated to second class. I was once stunned and hurt when a black American friend couldn't get served in a bar.

However, all was welcoming for this small (5'6") American, while my sense of love grew to passion. Bin-san was an artist whose deep eyes held me riveted, whose sword promised rape, but gay guys in Japan, I would learn, must get married and have children. Still, I would have stayed with Bin, stayed in Japan the rest of my life, if he'd have let me. Kenji-san was the rock writer, most popular boy in the Mejiro district. He introduced me to editors and served as translator and host of the crash-pad commune officially rented by his girlfriend, Reiko, and sister Yuko. We all pretended that only the girls lived there, for the benefit of their mother.

Mitsuyo was an improbable American Indian woman who'd married high lineage in Japan and became archery master to the Imperial family; her husband, Kenichi, was a university radical turned poet and philosopher/teacher. They taught me the old ways of calligraphy, Shinto beliefs, ritual tea ceremony, and riotous sake drinking long into the night.

Shobun Sha Publishers issued Japanese translations of my books, indecipherable wonders whose titles warped badly in the translation. *Cosmic Profit*, a book about U.S. entrepreneurs, became *How to Make Money Without a Job*. (Come to think of it, not a bad title. *Sold* better than the English-language original too.) A publisher in Tokyo is not remotely like one in New York. At Shobun Sha, they lined up the office staff and bowed to me, served drinks and snacks, and got everybody roaring drunk before discussing business. In New York the author is not some distinguished thinker worthy of profound respect, but just another freelancer scamming lunch.

The Japanese do business and life with an intensity that is downright frightening to the Western mind, however. Work is paramount, commitments are sacred, social courtesies are rigidly defined. You don't just stand someone up for a dinner invitation or turn up late for the office—they might, as they did for me, send the police out looking for you, worried that you'd committed suicide over some relatively insignificant *faux pas*. Japan is the only place I've found where death by one's own hand is considered good, noble, and right. (And horses run clockwise around the race track, baseball games end in a tie, books read from back to front, kids buy beer and liquor from public vending machines—*everything's backward*.)

After six months of turning Japanese, I was in grave danger of making a lifetime commitment to staying in Japan, but one thing nagged at me, the one thing still missing. The guru, the wise man, the lover, the light—where was the Buddha known as the Leader?

Slipping away on a Polish freighter, watching Yokohama mills and smokestacks grow smaller and smaller, I tore myself from the Honshu mainland bound for bad-ass Hong Kong and heroin, leaving behind Paul and Sachiko and, already, their offspring in utero. They were a picture of loving contentment; I was a self-conscious Siddhartha determined to walk the face of the earth until I found the secret of heart-be-stillness.

Hong Kong was no cousin to Japan, quite the opposite in many respects. It was dangerous, filled with criminality, compared to Japan's safety, and the shopkeepers and natives were always cheating and overpricing, compared to Japan's universal civic honesty. While drugs in Japan were severely prohibited and almost impossible to get, they were available in all the back alleys of Hong Kong. If self-mutilation is your style, the free port brings every imaginable vice to the table.

On Lantau Island, a short ferry ride from the city, I met one of the most peculiar characters on the path, Dr. A. Yow from South Carolina, traveling with two heavy trunks filled with an unpublished manuscript, *The Book of the Cosmos*. Dr. Yow was about sixty and the self-appointed director of the Society of the Cosmos, as well as its only member. As the only Americans on the island, we more or less gravitated to each other's company despite our age difference and although he stood somewhat aloof, declaring, "Loneliness is weakness."

His cosmology seemed rooted in bitter feelings toward the U.S. and rejection by the "straight" academic world, but Dr. Yow and I both enjoyed the experience of the Pi Lo monastery high atop the volcanic island. A rickety local bus snaked up the mountainside, carrying chickens and rice and perhaps mail to the monks hiding in caves, overlooking the South China Sea and the busy metropolis in the far distance. Lantau Island loomed serenely over the frenetic madness of Hong Kong; the monastery was exactly the sort of place I'd look for if I were indeed a monk, but no such luck.

Hong Kong didn't seem the place to find a master, but the last few days there were enjoyable enough. Long hair blowing in the wind, I hung off the end of the trolley cars and climbed the mountain overhanging this den of humanity seething on the South China Sea. A marijuana purchase turned into a frightening back-street taxi ride to hell, but the friendly opium pushers operated out of an alley behind the Bank of America, easy and open as you please to smoke "six pipes, fifty cents."

Promised money failed to appear at American Express. Kick a man when he's down. Better carry on to Bangkok, leaving a forwarding address, than wait in the Kong for what may or may not arrive, I thought, and that decision brought salvation and peace. Thailand is another universe completely, the land of smiles, humid steamy jungle of intrigue, greed, jabbering prostitutes, and sweet shop girls, lovely olive boys eager to serve, hot food for the spice in your soul, palm trees, and easy living.

A sense of euphoria rose up from the moment the plane touched down on the outskirts of the capital. This Bangkok smelled and looked old, an ancient throne city, not glistening with skyscrapers like Hong Kong or spewing technobabble like Tokyo. The favored transportation was a motorized rickshaw with two-person backseat under an umbrella and driver perched atop a loud moped engine bap-bapping crazily through the streets, dodging buses and cars and pedestrians. The hotel room was fifty cents a night, a good price for 1972. The women cooked fiery sauces in the lobby, where 7-Up over ice brought cool refreshment to the brow and constipation to the bowels (who knows what kinds of little parasites in the cubes?). No matter, the high from Thai made every day perfect, a lazy dream in a dangerous war zone.

Which is not to deny the deathly serious problems facing every Thai, from poverty and disease to breath-choking pollution and nearby gunfire. The insanely unmuffled traffic in Bangkok was fractious, aggressive, laughing in the face of death. The endless solicitations of bar girls and streetwalkers grew tedious and depressing. The boys were charming and sad-eyed, took me home to meet their mothers in floating boat houses, pounding laundry on river rocks. Wonderful people, easy to like and quick to embrace a traveler, the Thais were still dying young in an economy of scarcity.

Still, I renewed my visa again and again, reluctant to leave a country so full of love and strong marijuana. When the time finally came, I sadly took the night train to Penang on the Malay Peninsula. The following morning's newspaper carried a startling page-one photo and story: Bangkok police had raided the hippie hotel where I was staying and made off with my comrades. I'd missed being arrested by a few hours. Terrified and pale, I thanked whatever lucky stars were guiding me.

Penang was lost in a Muslim chant, all white sands and ivory, the fabulous wealth of Malaysian culture mingling uncomfortably with Chinese commerce. Malays and Chinese just plain don't like each other but coexist peacefully enough. The beach at Batu Feringhi became my home front; shelter was a rented room in a Chinese family home or an abandoned hut with Caliban houseman and fellow freaks Ben from Philly and Pyaro from Kathmandu. We played and smoked opium in Chinese dens and it was divine fun, but Penang was clearly not the final stop on the path, just a resting place and milestone, a port of departure to the motherland, *India*.

What is it about India that makes strong men weep, loose women become nuns, pacifists take up clubs, and soldiers lay down their arms? The place is overwhelming to every human instinct. Pity, horror, shame, awe, and astonishment were all commingled in the first sight of land from the deck of the decrepit passenger vessel *State of Madras*, which had carried me second-class in a mahogany bunk bed cabin from Penang. This is India, but *what is this*?

For sure, I figured, there had to be some wisdom in a place like that, where human misery was so intense that only a deep spirituality could make life worth living. Of course, the Indians themselves were more interested in acquiring my dollars, U.S.-made shirts, Japanese razor blades, ballpoint pens, whatever, any material things made outside India, any money not rupees, any little shard of comfort in a land of eternal want.

Aggressive street vendors, rickshaw drivers, black-market money changers dog the path of the Western visitor, and so much for the alleged sublimity of the Indian consciousness. Of course, certain priests and high Brahmins spoke warmly to me of Mother Kali and other religious matters, but those were exceptions to the street shriek of "Sahib, baksheesh!" Beggars everywhere. After viewing an Elvis Presley movie in a Calcutta theater, we stepped gingerly over the naked bodies of a mother and five children, sleeping in a circle on the sidewalk.

Choose your circle of hell: Madras, Calcutta, New Delhi, Bombay, Banaras, or Goa, they all steamed with leftover humanity and young visitors like myself, with knapsacks and dwindling funds, clubbing together in crash-pad urban dormitory rooms. Sleep on the floor till a bed comes open at Ma's Place, I learned. Aspirin is a black-market commodity because it really relieves pain. A ticket on a railroad train is a privilege worth fighting for in a mob of sweaty, pushing contenders. I clobbered a railroad conductor with an umbrella in a fit of pique after he hauled me off a second-class car. So this is enlightenment?

Then the worst happened, just as predicted by the orange-robed monk in some gone Bengal train station who read my palm and said, "Big name, little money. Soon all the money gone." Travelers checks stolen in Calcutta, I ran to American Express to claim my refund and was told it would take thirty days to get one. "What am I supposed to do in Calcutta without money for the next thirty days?" I screamed.

"That is your problem," the clerk replied. "You come from the richest country on earth, why don't you ask your countrymen for help?" There were no Americans at American Express, but I found a passle of 'em at the Salvation Army Hotel, where in fact they made a policy of extending credit (including meals) to foreigners waiting on refunds. So I wouldn't starve but also couldn't leave Calcutta and had to learn the way of Bengal. One Bengali is a poet, two Bengalis are a political party, three Bengalis are *two* political parties.

An Australian student crashing at the Salvation Army introduced us to new levels of hashish frenzy. "You look like you'd enjoy a good flogging," he said in a voice that induced terror and retreat in me. Who needs flogging when you're already dabbling in starvation, staph infection, and cow worship? Mango shakes made with local ice water assured a state of constant diarrhea, but we freaks couldn't get enough of the cold drinks in the wilting Indian heat. "You are a

Mungo, like a mango, but are you as sweet?" chimed the little old guru buying me tea and biscuits on the third-class train ride out of that country, out of India to the only place left on the map, Nepal, the mighty fortress of the north.

The first night in Kathmandu, it became clear to me that this end-of-the-road place would hold the key to my pilgrimage. Nepal would produce the answers to the cosmic questions and release me from my bond so I could return to the West. The place was holy, the people as destitute as the Indians but much happier and more accepting of their fate, philosophical even. In the early 1970s, Nepal attracted a large subculture of Western youth intent on searching for some greater meaning to life than our material roots had given us, as well as callow boys and girls wanting nothing more than the cheap life, endless legal hashish sold in public shops (my favorite, the Eden Hashish Centre), and local crafts and rugs to be resold at a profit in the States. Kathmandu was our grand free ride, a literal paradise for the counterculture wayfarer.

Here also my money expired completely. I wrote a letter to Cynthia Williams, a friend from Carmel, California, who had once rented me a writer's cabin on the Big Sur coast, asking for a loan of fifty dollars to get me back to Calcutta, where I'd stashed three hundred dollars in a bank safe-deposit vault after getting my refund. It was enough to cover transportation back to Japan, where jobs and money are readily available. After mailing the letter, I just started walking up the mountain from Kathmandu, in the general direction of Mount Everest and Tibet, and walked that lonesome highway for weeks, subsisting on small meals and sleeping on floors in the homes of Nepalese peasants along the way, paying with clothing and personal items from my knapsack.

Day by day, my burden decreased until I owned nothing but a few loincloths and simple shirts, a pair of sandals, and a U.S. passport.

The crazy saint of Manigoan, Nepal, near the highest Himalayan peaks, found my body and spiritual quest hilarious. He wanted most of all to experience New York City, where, he had heard, they had tall buildings and many cold drinks. You're not a monk, so be a householder, he told me; go home and be glad.

Home wasn't as far away as all that. By the time I got back to Kathmandu, the U.S. embassy was celebrating the Fourth of July with a hot-dog-and-beer picnic, open free of charge to anyone with a U.S. passport. Undernourished, barely dressed, wide-eyed at the incredible wealth of food and drink flown in from America on an airplane, I was nonetheless an American, admitted to the feast and happy for it.

At the American Express mail drop, a large stack of letters waited for me. Cynthia had mailed copies of my letter around to various friends in the U.S., and a heartening stack of fifty-dollar international money orders was my reward, an actual king's ransom big enough to take all my hotel mates out to dinner, pay off all old room bills to the sweet little boys at the Match Box (the only hotel in the world completely managed by ten-year-olds), buy a one-way sailing ticket to Singapore and Tokyo and souvenir gifts for all.

Japan was, the second time around, too much like home to be exotic. I was forced out after an unfortunate bust. A friend was arrested in Kyoto with some Thai weed I'd given him and sentenced to a year in jail. At the insistence of friends I went into hiding and eventually caught a Norwegian freighter to Canada, another wind-tossed crossing but happier alone than with Paul Williams the year before because my year-plus wandering around in Asia had dramatically *changed my mind*. Love is a conceit, an idea whose time hasn't come yet, I learned; the important thing is, *what's for dinner?*

Paul and Sachiko had in the meantime moved to New York City, where he'd rented a loft at 77 Franklin Street, way downtown south of Houston Street, using my last three thousand dollars from book royalties as a down payment. New York and Tokyo are the only places I know where it costs a fortune to "buy" a rental unit, and today's prices would be considerably more than three grand in "key money."

Anyway, I moved into the loft while Sachiko was in the late stages of pregnancy with their first child, despite the warnings of concerned friends that an ex-boyfriend should *not* move in with a newlywed couple. There was trouble right away and all the time. Paul's mother minced no words in voicing her disapproval of the faggot from his past. Sachiko more or less screamed at Paul all the time; she was miserably unhappy in America, spoke no English, was afraid to go outside and put off by the rudeness of New Yorkers.

Meanwhile, Paul had introduced me to an astrologer from Long Island, a woman who had an infant daughter, had recently left her third husband, and promptly informed me that I was to be the fourth. She had seen a fortune teller, an uptown psychic, who predicted my coming, and she was waiting for me. She said we were destined to have a kid together. "I'm sure you've got the wrong guy," I said. "I'm gay and living with Paul."

"That's all right, you'll see," Crystal responded. "I'll be here when you need to come to me."

She sold her furniture and moved from Long Island to a sublet apartment in Greenwich Village from which she could call me daily with offers of love and companionship. Paul had mandated a no-smoking policy in the loft (no smoking tobacco, that is), and Crystal would call to say "I'm around the corner in a bar with a full pack of Nat Shermans" just when the nicotine urge had reached its foulest peak.

Paul was starting a magazine called *Rallying Point* and needed help getting it off the ground, while Crystal insisted we should get together and have this fabled child, this wunderkind foretold. They got into a violent argument over it at the Chelsea Hotel one evening when we attended a party for Allen Ginsberg and William S. Burroughs. It was flattering, in a way, to be the desired party, the prize under contest, but I wished the astrologer would give up and go away.

She finally left the city, kid in tow, after spending more

than four thousand dollars in a month of pursuing me all over New York. She went back to Long Island to house-sit a friend's place in Belport, swearing that one fine night I'd join her there. And of course I did—on a snowy January evening after Paul and I had quarreled so fiercely he threw me down the stairs. It was the middle of the night and I was too embarrassed to call friends, so I walked along avenues covered with a light dusting of snow, crunching my foot-steps into virgin frozen tundras, all the way to Penn Station at Thirty-fourth Street, which offered heat and shelter from the storm.

Sitting there shivering in the great-ceilinged station waiting room, I heard the p.a. announcer bring the news that the lengthy Long Island Railroad strike had been settled at the negotiating table. The first train to Long Island in months would leave in thirty minutes! I called Crystal, even though it was 4 A.M. She picked up the phone saying, "I knew you'd call. When are you arriving?" "Five-ten at the Belport station."

We started drinking champagne in the predawn mist, kitchen windows steamed up from the hissing radiator, the moon was full in Virgo, one thing led to another and bam— "It's a boy!" my mantra chanted in my head, while she insisted a girl would come from conception under a feminine moon sign. We both knew, without doubt, that egg and sperm had collided successfully, instantly, the room was spinning and the moon winking as pink dawn colored the horizon.

Late the following day . . . Waking in Belport, Long Island (where am I?), and realizing the full impact of what had happened, I tempered the instinct to escape with the reality of no place to run to. The witch lady cast her spell and I was a goner, lost in her ovulatory web at least until the progeny should arrive. Married with children overnight, I marveled at her baby daughter, sitting in her high chair, rapping her spoon and chanting, "I love you, Raymos!"

This same daughter had doting grandparents in the New York area, a hospital administrator and his wife who were good for sizable checks even though their son (and only child) was no longer living with Crystal. The baby was their only grandchild and sweet comfort of their old age. These grandparents mustn't know about our impending child, Crystal reasoned, because she was not yet divorced from her daughter's father, only separated a few months, and didn't want to lose the financial support of the grandparents. We had to leave New York to have our baby, but where to go?

I had some friends down in Costa Rica living on a commune devoted to Gurdjieffian thinking and astral projection. It sounded far enough, all right, to escape her daughter's family. She'd just tell them in postcards and letters that she and the baby were on a trip. We took a train to New Orleans and flew out of there to Mexico on the first leg of a nightmare journey to Latin America and voodoo nights. The authorities, after studying our passports, noticed that I was not the father of the little girl and asked to see written consent from the child's natural father giving permission for his kid to be taken out of the U.S.

"He's dead," Crystal said. And somehow got away with it. She killed him herself at the New Orleans airport.

From Mexico City to Oaxaca, Guatemala, Honduras, Nicaragua, and Costa Rica we traveled on dusty, shockless local buses, like the holy family turned away from every home, on the lam. The baby grew fatter in Crystal's stomach, but she slipped in the shower in Mexico and dislocated her back. Constant pain and trips to doctors' offices plagued our journey. Every stop involved collecting money desperately begged from friends in the U.S. and wired by Western Union or AmEx. We passed through Managua, Nicaragua, just after a devastating earthquake had leveled the city and were lucky to find a dismal room in a shack on the outskirts of town. The place looked like the aftermath of nuclear war. We finally landed in San José, Costa Rica, on Good Friday, in time to see the *penitentes* wailing in the streets.

The people at the commune proved nice enough, but the place was primitive and we didn't feel at home there.

Crystal's medical condition required better health care than we could find in Central America—the astrologer was also into New Age health techniques, unknown south of the border. So we wound up flying to Seattle, of all places, simply because we had a friend there who was studying to be a naturopathic doctor. The National College of Naturopathic Medicine was based in Seattle, a pleasant city of lakes and waterways and endless rain, which in 1973 was in the throes of a massive depression. Empty houses were for sale in every neighborhood, abandoned by mortgagees who couldn't keep up their payments. Billboards pronounced, "Will the last person to leave Seattle please turn off the lights."

But it provided safe harbor for our destined child, a boy named Phoenix born in a simple pinewood clinic in Lynnwood, Washington, delivered by a doctor named Gold.

For the first three years of his life, Phoenix and I were more or less always together, as I changed diapers and made bottles while his mother worked at her astrology, did charts for clients, and attended her evening classes. At this point in the early 1970s the term *househusband* hadn't been coined, but I was certainly glad to be one. Phoenix and his older sister were the guiding lights of my life, angels come from heaven to protect me from my own self-destructive instincts. Once you have kids, you're not allowed to be crazy or broke anymore.

After our marriage broke up, however, Crystal and I went down widely different roads. She eventually moved to Michigan, while I headed south to California. Phoenix and his sister visited me many summers and vacation periods, for as long as six weeks at a time, and those were riotously happy occasions. But the noncustodial parent simply misses out on the "real" job and joy of raising the kids.

My son today is sixteen and still his father's pride: he is the editor, publisher, and one-man production department of his own small magazine, and it's radical as can be. *MonkeyWrench* is in the spirit of Edward Abbey's books and the philosophy of social disruption. Famous long ago again!

Chapter 6
Welcome to the Hotel California

SEATTLE TURNED AROUND in the five years I spent there, from a depressed city without jobs or prospects to a boom town rising up proud, Queen City of the Pacific Northwest, everybody's candidate for most livable. The city provided a good deal of free culture, the arts commission supported local writers, the weather was miserably wet but seldom freezing, and, hey, our group of friends (mostly all refugees from other parts of the nation) considered ourselves smart and lucky to live in the Evergreen State.

The marriage fell apart promptly, but I suppose it wasn't meant to survive any kind of long haul. Astrologer and author parted ways bitterly, with a nasty custody battle for the child, but it's all blood under the dam, as Albee wrote in *Who's Afraid of Virginia Woolf? The kids are all right*, they always say, but who knows how deeply divorce affects them? The kids are victims, but the grown-ups are too.

With a couple of partners, I owned a bookstore and small-press publishing enterprise called Montana Books, and many are the legends of that place still floating around

Seattle. Montana Books was as close to literary heaven as
we're permitted to get: a reader's bookstore with plants,
light, coffee, music, readings and parties and seminars at
night, a university, a church.

We were the original distributors of a book called *Dry
It, You'll Like It* by Gen MacManiman, the first book on
drying foods in a home dehydrator. It has sold at least four
hundred thousand copies by now and is still in print. We
also republished Aldous Huxley's landmark book *The Art of
Seeing*, which had been out of print for some time. The
rights cost us only $500 in advance. It had wide popularity
in the 1940s, when the Bates Method of improving vision
without glasses reached its peak in this country, but both
method and book had fallen out of favor. We correctly
reasoned that the new generation of health-conscious alter-
native-culture vultures would scoop it up. That one has
probably sold about forty thousand copies and is still in
print.

The Art of Seeing also gave me the chance to meet
Laura Archera Huxley, Aldous's widow, who is very much
alive and sizzling with new ideas in the alabaster Mulhol-
land Drive hilltop residence they shared in Hollywood. She
is the author of *You Are Not the Target* and *This Timeless
Moment*, wonderful books, and carries on the progressive
ideals in her late years.

Montana Books eventually spawned two other bookstores, but I left Seattle in 1978, abandoning the enterprise
to my partners, burned out on business management (never
my strong suit). I did learn from the experience that independent booksellers operate on such a thin margin it's remarkable they can make a living at all. Christmas is extravagant in the average bookstore, but the rest of the year you
have to sell T-shirts and croissants to pay the rent.

Moving to California from the Northwest is as easy as
letting go; somehow the road south is a long, downhill
slide, while the northward trek is a climb against gravity. En
route to an ultimate fall, all the way into Hollywood, I

caught on to a coastal shelf in the little community of
Carmel on the Montery Peninsula, famed home of artists,
writers, and Clint Eastwood. The same Cynthia Williams
who'd rescued me from Nepal rented me a cabin, and I swam
with the dolphins and Point Lobos sea lions.

What a place is the Monterey-Carmel area! It's taken up
many a book of its own. The neighborhood of the Carmel
Highlands, where Cynthia reigns as matron of the Carmel
Highlands Institute, contains some of the most historic
Greene and Greene castles from the turn of the century and
some of the wildest characters of the west. Down the coast
a spit from my little house lived neighbors Daniel and Lilith
James in one of those G and G stone mansions, inherited
from Dan's father, D. L. James, a noted Kansas City indus-
trialist.

What made Dan James different from your average senior citizen aristocrat living in a Carmel castle was that he'd
been a wild radical as a youth and a Communist in the
1930s, married Lilith (a dancer) and with her wrote the
Broadway musical *Bloomer Girl*, worked with Chaplin on
The Great Dictator, sheltered Billie Holiday from the feds,
got called before the House Un-American Activities Committee in the big McCarthy Red scare and *refused to name
names*.

Blackballed from the industry and the writing trade
forever, Dan James couldn't get work under his own name so
he adopted the pseudonym Danny Santiago in honor of the
Chicano culture that he and Lilith embraced in L.A. Although wealthy, they were always running with the *comadres*
and *compadres*, you see. And as Danny Santiago, James hit it
big, winning the *Redbook* Award for short stories and the
Rosenthal Award of the American Academy of Arts and
Sciences for the novel *Famous All Over Town*, a charming
coming-of-age story about a fourteen-year-old boy and his
Mexican family in east L.A.

Trouble was nobody knew that *Famous All Over Town*
was not written by a Latino, not even the publisher (Simon
& Schuster) and James's agent, Carl Brandt. Danny Santi-

ago was presumed to be an up-and-coming Hispanic writer, but of course James could not appear in person to receive his awards and lost a Pulitzer Prize nomination because he couldn't produce evidence of Santiago's birth.

The Pulitzer Prize committee requires a date and place of birth for an author to be nominated, James's editor Bob Bender told me, and of course Dan could provide neither without blowing his cover. Simon & Schuster, although eager to nominate the book for the prize, couldn't prove the author even existed.

Aside from those of us in the neighborhood who knew the dark secret of Danny Santiago, the only other writers in on it were Joan Didion and John Gregory Dunne, friends of the Jameses who had bought their house in L.A. when the couple moved north to retire in Carmel. And it was Dunne who finally talked James into letting him expose the secret in the *New York Review of Books* in 1984. The ensuing media exposure was nothing short of phenomenal. James/Santiago was on page one of the *New York Times*, in the People pages of all the magazines, and on every television network. Some *real* Hispanic writers were outraged, and a fierce controversy ensued.

(I was even accused of being Danny Santiago myself, more than once. The fiction editor of *Esquire* found it curious that Santiago and Mungo lived in the same town and that I'd served as liaison between Santiago and his publisher in New York on several occasions and that I was the only one who claimed to know Santiago personally. Besides, he said, I wrote *Famous Long Ago* and Santiago wrote *Famous All Over Town*, as if there was some dark significance to the similarity in titles.)

Across the street lived Ephraim Doner and his wife, Rosa, living legends of Carmel who are famous for knowing everybody who ever passed through, including D. H. Lawrence, Henry Miller, Jack Kerouac, Linus Pauling, Joan Baez—oh, the list is endless.

"The future is not what it used to be," Doner laughed.

He and Rosa are both eighty-three now. "All of my future is like my hair—in a box!" He flung his arms into the air, gestured to the panorama outside his home above Point Lobos, and added reassuringly, "Don't worry, though, we'll always be right here, haunting this place!"

Doner is a painter and ceramicist whose tiles and oils are collected in the homes of celebrities and nowadays bring a handsome price; Rosa ran the "little red schoolhouse" on the Carmel beach for twenty-five years and raised several generations of Carmel youngsters. And an evening at the Doners is still a divine whirlwind of rich conversation, gourmet food, fine wines, laughter and argument in multiple languages, Ping-Pong, and poetry, as it has been for forty years and thousands of guests.

"He is absolutely unique, undiluted, integral," Henry Miller wrote about Doner in his book *My Bike and Other Friends* (1978). "English is too dull, too flat, too weak to render his nature, his soul. For all of the friends and acquaintances I have had, he is the only one with a predominant soul. Chassidic as he is, he is always whirling about you, snapping his fingers and muttering prayers. He makes one dizzy immediately. Dizzy, thirsty, and talkative. For he is an electrifier!

"He always knows more than one is supposed to know about everything."

Doner likes to say, "I've tried to be not only obscure but *nationally* obscure!" He didn't succeed too well. Kenneth Rexroth wrote about him. He was there when Ferlinghetti and Rexroth coined the word *beatnik*. ("I added the Russian part," he said. Doner was born in a part of Russia that is now Poland and came here via Paris and New York in the 1920s.) Robert Creeley, Allen Ginsberg, Edward Dahlberg, Ansel Adams, John Steinbeck, and others drank his wine and quoted his jokes.

Often asked for his philosophy of life, Doner offered this: "I start with Hillel's philosophy: 'If I am not for myself, who will be for me? If I am only for myself, who am I? If not now, when?' Then I add my mother's philosophy of life: 'It's all the fault of Columbus!' My mother hated this country. We lived in a small, cold apartment in New York, and we kids knew she was serious when she hollered 'Columbus!' To that I have to add only one thing: 'If they give, take. If they take, *yell!*' "

About Clint Eastwood, what can one say that hasn't already appeared in the *National Enquirer* or one of the other tabloids? This guy, a longtime Carmel neighbor, attracts more publicity than any living local since John Steinbeck, whose portrait is blazoned on every imaginable restaurant, inn, magazine, T-shirt, and tourist guide. Eastwood, when he was mayor of Carmel for two years, unwillingly spawned a whole retail industry (called Clintville, it operates out of a tourist-trap shop on the main drag, Ocean Avenue) of souvenirs bearing his name and likeness. When the pope came to town, we had to endure strange yahoos from Cleveland and Poughkeepsie walking around in shirts reading, "Thou hast made my day!"

Just to get in on a piece of the action and throw a little dada into the scene, we published a bright red bumper sticker that said, "Save Carmel—IMPEACH CLINT." This was meant as a joke more than a serious political campaign, but in no time *USA Today* picked up the item on page one of its Life section: "Author Ray Mungo is trying to throw Dirty Harry out of town." Lord, the mail orders for those bumper stickers came flooding in from all over the country and world.

Of course, it was zany nonsense, and after the furor died down we didn't bother to reprint the bumper stickers, but there is still a secret cache of them hidden in Carmel and if you want one, write to me at P.O. Box 8914, Palm Springs, California 92263, and I'll see what I can do.

Eastwood stepped out of politics but still owns a couple of popular restaurants around town and vast land holdings he manipulates to his imperial ends. Often seen with actress Sondra Locke before they broke up in 1989, he steps out into society but should be thanked for staying out of town as much as possible. Some wag erected a sign at the gates of the town: "Clint's Not Here." It didn't do any good, and now Carmel's about as expensive and crowded (particularly in summer) as Hollywood itself, although surely a different and better world.

Robert Redford gave me my first taste of Hollywood back in 1970 when he purchased the film option on *Famous Long Ago*, but Redford is in a class by himself. Bankable as he is, he doesn't need to live in Los Angeles or even California but operates out of his Sundance ranch in Utah and generously supports good causes for the environment and development of promising young filmmakers. When he bought the rights to *Famous*, however, the film industry had made only a couple of efforts to capture the counterculture generation, and they were ghastly failures. *The Strawberry Statement* descended to a scene where a college boy gets a blow job from a pretty coed as his reward for participating heroically in a demonstration, while *Wild in the Streets* portrayed a highly unrealistic, out-of-control kind of youth fascism, rounding up "old" people (over thirty) into concentration camps and so forth. It was just plain stupid stuff and didn't show our side to advantage, and I didn't want such a film made from my precious book.

Redford was gracious enough to let me attempt a script—although it came out badly—and for a year or so I was embroiled with agents and producers but, as usually happens with options, the film was never made. No blame, we parted amicably. And when I finally moved to Hollywood in 1982, the reputation of that unproduced film still lingered there.

In late 1981, I'd met the Japanese boy of my dreams in Carmel, but he wasn't *Japanese* Japanese. He was *Hollywood* Japanese sansei, more American than the Fourth of July, this Robear Yamaguchi. He led us to the gates of Tinseltown like Moses parting the Red Sea, and we lucked into the most extraordinary house we've ever shared. Seems that Alicia Bay Laurel, author of the bestseller *Living on the Earth* and herself a mother to all gay guys, introduced us to James Leo

Herlihy, the great author of *Midnight Cowboy*, *All Fall Down*, *Blue Denim*, and other fine novels successfully transferred to the screen.

Herlihy, ruggedly handsome and lean in his fifties, had a spectacular home in the Silver Lake neighborhood of L.A., with panoramic views from the big Hollywood sign on the hill to the ocean at Santa Monica and the San Bernardino mountains to the east. This elegant retreat on Landa Street was offered to us for the token rent of $1,000 a month (had it been a hotel, it'd be that much a day), complete with swimming pool and pool boy to maintain it, while "Jamie" exiled himself in Greece, recharging creative batteries.

James Leo Herlihy was one of my heroes, an author whose plays and movies I had revered. He wrote one of the best lines in English: "Don't look for a lover, be one." Living in his house was like being inside his soul, a fine and noble one. The late Jim Kirkwood, creator of *A Chorus Line*, came by and took us all off to a belly-dancing café for wicked gossip and passable couscous. Anybody could drop in at the Casa Landa; Truman, Tennessee, and all the boys knew the spot.

Ah, but operating in the Hollywood schmaze is just exactly what you'd expect, exhausting and demoralizing. I spent a good deal of time having lunch with studio executives who promised to fly Antonioni over to direct, and be in production for cable, and make me a star—God, they really talk that way—yet nothing ever got accomplished. They call you sweetheart, darling, and lover one day and won't take your phone calls the next.

That's a generalization, of course. I also met and dealt with good people, themselves trying to make sense out of the madness in the entertainment industry. Agent Paul Yamamoto from International Creative Management became a kind of guardian angel, arranging meetings and cashing checks for me. Producer Harvey Kahn at ITC in Studio City fed my body and soul and pursued the *Famous Long Ago* story long after Bob Redford's agent, Claire Deneger, had given up on it. Actor David Lander, who played Squiggy on "Laverne and Shirley," was a baseball buddy. *Los Angeles*

Times book editor Art Seidenbaum and *Playgirl* magazine editor Zina Klapperman kept me supplied with assignments.

The hard reality nonetheless is that many of L.A.'s promising actors, actresses, scriptwriters, and directors can be found waiting tables on Melrose Avenue or slouching on street corners along Santa Monica Boulevard, hoping to get lucky. Like any big city, L.A. is tough around the edges and no place to be if you're a stranger without cash. The industry, the entertainment business, is notorious for its instability, lying, thieving, and bankruptcy. All is truly vanity in this Hollywood illusion. It doesn't take long to see through the mask once you know the rules of the game. Your projects are always "in development." You "take" meetings and lunches and stay by a phone at all times.

And, if you're good at "pitching," you can make a fine living writing screenplays that never get produced, yet getting paid better for each new one.

It was a cushy life in the privacy and lavish comforts of Herlihy's enclave. The late, sainted author Anaïs Nin had been one of Jamie's friends and had stayed in the house; a beautiful oil portrait of her was mounted in the kitchen foyer and reproduced on postcards Herlihy used for personal correspondence. I knew that syndicated astrologer Sydney Omarr had once been in love with Anaïs Nin, so I mailed him a postcard and it served as a perfect device for gaining admission to his inner circle.

Omarr held court of a Sunday evening in his suite overlooking the Pacific at Santa Monica. The walls of his study were lined with photographs of movie stars and other celebrities with Omarr. Mae West literally asked him to come up and see her. Angie Dickinson is a big fan, Marilyn Monroe was dedicated to astrology, and Omarr told all about Nancy Reagan's addiction to her horoscope long before it made the newspapers. Seems Nancy and Merv Griffin have the same birthday and call each other every year to compare horoscopes, he said.

Frail and afflicted with multiple sclerosis, Omarr cannot venture much beyond his secure fortress. He is the astrologer's astrologer, stargazer to the stars; literally mil-

lions of people depend on him for daily advice in the newspaper. I asked him if that responsibility ever troubled him,
and he said it does bring trouble. Omarr gets crank calls
from people convinced that his horoscope column has some
personal meaning for them, and a husband once threatened
to shoot him for allegedly seducing his wife through the
newspaper. She was so convinced Omarr wanted to marry
her that she left home in New Jersey and set out to find him
in California.

He loves women, has been married and divorced several
times, and vied with Henry Miller for the affections of
Gloria Swanson. Women love Omarr too; they gather
around him and hang on his every word.

He likes nothing better than entertaining the beautiful
people with cocktail parties overlooking the sea, casting his
gaze around the room and making startling pronounce-
ments. "You've survived a great deal already. You've survived
things that would have killed other people," he told me
immediately upon meeting—as if he could read that in my
eyes.

"And you'll survive a lot more. You'll survive *everything*," he added.

RM: How would you describe what you do as a professional
astrologer?
SO: I interpret and interpolate the ephemerides and also use
a numerical technique. One leading astrologer said that
"Sydney Omarr is a general leading an army of the
superstitious."
RM: How did you get started in the business?
SO: At a very young age, about fourteen, in Philadelphia I
thought that astrology and palmistry and numbers were
tricks to add to my repertoire as a magician. I lied to the
American Guild of Variety Artists, saying I was eighteen, so I could perform. But when I began to look into
astrology, I saw there was a great deal to it.

I was also a journalist, and the combination of the
journalism and the magic made me a real skeptic, so I'm
more skeptical than the average person. Good astrolo-

gers are perceptive because they have to know history, astronomy, mathematics as well.

RM: Did Marilyn Monroe consult astrology?

SO: She was very interested, yes.

RM: What can you tell us about Mae West?

SO: Well, a fellow reporter named Leo Guild who was a friend of hers approached me and said, "Mae West would like you to come up and see her." She lived in Santa Monica at that time. When I walked in, the place was empty except for a chimpanzee working out on the parallel bars. Then a man appeared at the head of the stairs and said, "Mae West would like you to come up and see her." It did seem like a movie.

When I walked into the room where he pointed, it was empty too, and she was hiding behind the door. She felt in awe or afraid of me. She had read my book *Thought Dial* and some of the other things I had written. But when we talked, it turned out that both she and Mary Pickford were intensely interested in what Aldous Huxley used to call the mantic arts and sciences— psychic phenomena, mediumship, astrology, and so forth.

RM: Did Aldous Huxley invent the term *mantic arts*?

SO: No, you could look it up. It means divinatory arts. I did a documentary called *The Strange World of Psychic Phenomena*, and everyone was amazed when Aldous agreed to come on the program, and his widow, Laura, tells me she still uses *Thought Dial* in her home to locate lost articles and answer personal questions.

RM: What was Henry Miller really like?

SO: I wouldn't say Miller was rowdy or boisterous; in fact, he was rather quiet and basically modest. Only twice did I hear him use a four-letter word synonymous with love; once was with Kim Novak, the other time with Gloria Swanson. Gloria Swanson served dinner, and there was no wine on the table; Henry said, "Where the fuck is the wine?" She reached under the table and rang a bell, and it was served. With Kim Novak, I had done some astrological work for her, and she asked Henry, "What can I do for him?" and Henry said, "Give him a good fuck."

RM: Tell us how you met Anaïs Nin and what kind of relationship you had with her.

SO: Well, I fell in love with Anaïs Nin too, as well as Gloria Swanson. I met her through astrology, of course. She'd been with Jung and some of the other new psychiatrists, and in those days astrology was the darling of the intellectuals. She knew more about her sign, Pisces, than anyone else. Her diaries helped me a lot in my various so-called love affairs.

RM: Would you say you'd affected the history of movies or the course of literature?

SO: I affected the course of literature mainly because I gave Henry Miller the green light to publish his *Tropics* books in this country. As for the movies, well . . . Alan Jay Lerner became a fan of mine, and when they were filming *On a Clear Day You Can See Forever* he convinced them as a publicity thing to have me on the set.

RM: Did you ever have any contact with Ronald Reagan? Is it true the Reagans are interested in astrology?

SO: Yes, of course. The first contact I had in connection with Ronald Reagan—there was an old astrological researcher in Hollywood whose name now escapes me, but he was a bookworm who gave very few readings. He was scholarly. And when he died, among his papers was found a note that said, "Be in at 3 P.M. for my horoscope," signed by Ronald Reagan. Then I did an interview show where one of Reagan's press people told me of his interest in astrology. I did many shows with Merv Griffin, and he said that every July 6, which is Nancy's birthday as well as Merv's, Nancy would call him and they'd discuss their horoscopes.

RM: Tell us about the Kennedys.

SO: Well, John Kennedy was elected during the Jupiter-Saturn conjunction, and I got a quote, but it was third-hand, that he said, "I know about the jinx, but I'm going to break it." My connections to the Kennedys were through Gloria Swanson—she was with the father—and Angie Dickinson, who was with John. Susan

Strasbourg is another; she was a roommate of Marilyn Monroe for a while because Marilyn studied with her father, Lee Strasbourg, and Marilyn was with both John and Bobby. . . . Marilyn as a Gemini wanted to be compared only with Walt Whitman, Queen Victoria, and Ralph Waldo Emerson; she didn't want to be put in the class of common Geminis, only the famous intellectual ones.

RM: Do the stars ask your advice on a personal level or about their careers primarily?

SO: Everybody, whether a celebrity or not, asks for advice in this order: love, money or career, fitness or health.

Comes a time in Hollywood Lobotomy Space when you wake up in the morning realizing you'll scream if you have to talk to one more agent who calls his clients "baby." You'll die if you have to drive Beverly Boulevard to ICM and the Hughes Market one more time at three in the morning when the starlets are out, squeezing the avocados and sniffling. You'll go straight to hell if you have to lie and jive and pretend to respect some bozo whose idea of artistry is a TV sitcom aimed at a ten-year-old's sense of humor. You'll never laugh again unless you can get out of town.

With Jamie returning from Greece, we had to move anyway. Rather than take a depressing apartment, a long decline from the quality of Casa Landa, we figured we might as well blow town, try to escape the creeping meatball. At that moment, in some burst of fate, a letter arrived from novelist Warren Dearden in Haiku, Maui, saying that his wife needed to take a master's degree program in Boston, so the family would spend a year on the mainland. Did I know anyone interested in renting their furnished two-bedroom house in Haiku for a year? The rent was $375, and the place came with macadamia-nut trees, banana groves, lush garden, Maui Wowee, small Toyota, color TV, Siamese cat, and no hassles. Paradise on the cheap. Good-bye to the Hotel California, hello pakololo jungle-bunny island in the deep blue sea!

Chapter 7
If You Likea Ukulele Lady, Ukulele Lady Likea You

HOT AND HUMID WINDS blew across the open-air passenger terminal at Kahului Airport on da island of Maui,
and who the hell decided to make the Hawaiian Islands a
state of the union? The minute you land on Maui, you *know*
you're not in the United States anymore. This is a Polynesian
island lost in the middle of a vast South Pacific, thousands
of miles from any land mass, rich in ancient culture and
languages, and simply colonized by the white man in recent
times.

Civilization didn't particularly improve Hawaii. The
natives, who had never known illness or disease, were deci-
mated by European viruses. A common cold might be fatal.
Then big agricultural interests arrived—sugar and pineapples—until the people were reduced to working the fields
and no longer owned the land of their ancestors. Today,
Hawaii has a population one-third Polynesian or partly so
(every kine racial mix, brah), another third Japanese, and
the last third Caucasian. Only the very rich can afford to buy
land, but the resident population is poor and ill-educated,
close to the bottom of federal standards in every category.
Life is not easy or luxurious for most Hawaiians; jobs are
few and living expenses high.

Jim Jordan, one of the original commune members at Total Loss Farm in Vermont, had become a Zen monk and gardener on Maui and met us at the airport in his funky orange Volkswagen with bomber rolled and cold beer popping. People on Maui consider it normal and perfectly all right to drive a car while sipping cold beer from a can. It's hot, brah. We achieved a condition of tropical paralysis euphoria (TPE) while rolling along the eye-popping coast road with fabulous scenic beaches and lush jungle flowers.

But the first sight of the house in Haiku—*our* new house—shocked us back to reality. It was steaming decay, a little grass shack. Gecko lizards scampered around on the walls and across the ceiling over our bed—*eek*. Spiders big enough to challenge household pets slithered around, and every kine bug and flying insect knew no difference between indoors and out. This was jungle living, and we were unprepared.

Living in Haiku, on the wet side of the island and far from the tourist meccas of Lahaina and sleek beachfront hotels at Kaanapali, was nothing akin to a tourist experience. The neighbor was an enormous Samoan wrestler type with wife and nobody could ever figure how many children, including a retarded eleven-year-old daughter who ran around the yard in diapers, six dogs, and a six hundred-pound pig that occasionally got loose and terrorized the whole neighborhood. Shortly after we'd moved in, we met the giant from next door at 2 A.M., when he appeared in our screen door, looming large and frightening in the moonlight. He smiled and held out a joint. "You likea smoke?"

Hey, we likea smoke, no baddah you. Anything he liked, we liked, especially at that hour and considering his huge frame and apparently drunken condition. "No baddah you" is pidgin English for "Don't let it bother you." Maui people don't speak English precisely but a pidgin dialect that is sometimes unintelligible to the mainland ear.

"My pig get loose, run aroun' yo' macadamia trees, no baddah you, OK?"

"Hey, no baddah *us*."

"My wife, she yell and scream at me, maybe I scream at

her, sometimes got to hit the kids, they screaming—no baddah you, no baddah me."

"No baddah us!"

"But sometimes you don't got gas, you need a ride to town, you come to me, OK? I give you food, I give you ride to town, whatever you need, come to my house, I give you. No baddah me. OK?"

And so forth. He turned out to be a pleasant enough fellow, and when he roasted the entire pig in a giant hole in the ground, we were invited to the feast. But as city slickers from L.A., we could barely understand the words coming out of his mouth.

Our version of paradise diminished the first time we went grocery shopping and reeled from the prices. Because Hawaii's so damn far away, anything from the mainland costs a lot more, sometimes double. But even the local produce, milk, bread, staples like that, were insanely overpriced by mainland standards. How can people here afford to eat at these prices, we wondered?

The answer was they couldn't and didn't. They lived off what fell from the trees and burst from the vine in their own and their neighbors' back yards. Little kids came to our porch saying, "My mama says kin we pick up macadamia nuts in yo' yard?" (We always said yes.) "My mama says kin we have some banana?" Of course, or they'll rot on the stalk. The local politicians even fed the whole town during election campaigns, competing with each other to throw the biggest luau. The mayor of Maui provided a sit-down dinner for three thousand; an open bar serving beer, wine, and spirits; dancing to an orchestra and swaying-hipped hula girls. We ate out every night on a different politician's tab, disregarding his party or platform.

Except for the tourist industry, hotels and restaurants and such, there's not much viable economy on Maui. I registered to be a substitute teacher of English at the local high school, but the principal gave me fair warning not to expect many students. "English is their least favorite subject, man, and when da surf comes up, no boys at all will be in class and only a few girls." I wrote a column for the *Maui Reporter*, a kind of first-impressions or newcomer feature, describing Maui through the eyes of a visitor. That paid twenty-five dollars a week. We recycled aluminum cans discarded by tourists, combing the beaches for the precious metals redeemable for ten or fifteen bucks, dinner money.

Communication with the mainland was eternally frustrating and difficult. It was seven hours later in New York, so by the time I'd had morning coffee and sat down to work at 10 A.M., it was already the end of the business day back East and too late to call an editor. If I reached an editor, he or she would usually be so jealous that I was living on Maui that I wouldn't get the assignment or check. *Playgirl* magazine bought some Hawaiian-oriented theme pieces and now and then I could sell a travel article, but on the whole it was rather like trying to do business with a foreign country. The local banks in Kahului all had a policy of placing a hold on deposits from mainland checks for two weeks; they'd been burned too often.

I took up ghostwriting the memoirs of an elderly lady in Wailuku who had about as much chance of getting them published as I did of winning a surfing contest, which is to say none. The only healthy business on da island was the marijuana trade, and the only jobs available were for at-home bud clippers. For eight dollars an hour and all the pot you could smoke, you sat home all day clipping the bud from the leaf and packaging Maui Wowee for shipment to the mainland. The authorities were always trying to thwart these shipments, but the growers managed to stay a jump ahead and the vast majority of the stuff got through. You got the feeling that nobody in Hawaii took marijuana use or growing very seriously. Grass is available everywhere in the islands; total strangers will approach you on the beach with joints for sale.

The growers had devised extremely clever ways to avoid detection. They walked into overgrown jungle clearings, drip-irrigated with piping and hand-carried water, even grew potted plants in the highest limbs of trees to provide air cover. Although too poor to buy the stuff, we often received gift joints from friends and generally stayed high on Maui, which was of course part of the problem of living there. You smoke that crazy reefer and all ambition goes right down the drain.

One day I actually went to the grocery store wearing underpants and nothing else. They were boxer shorts, thin enough to be revealing, and in my mentally loose condition I suppose I must have thought I had bathing trunks on. It wasn't until I was standing in line at Fukushima's neighborhood store in Haiku, waiting to pay for my two-dollar loaf of bread and a dollar quart of milk, that I looked down and realized with horror, *I'm out in public barefoot and practically naked.* But, typical of Maui, nobody noticed, or if they did, it no baddah them.

It baddah me, however, to the point that I thought I'd better get off that island while I still had any semblance of mind left.

Things weren't all bad on Maui, not by a long stretch. Alicia Bay Laurel, the same author who'd introduced us to Jamie Herlihy, also lived on the island and in fact had introduced me to Warren Dearden years earlier. Her royalties from the bestsellers *Living on the Earth* and *Being of the Sun* had trickled down to nothing, but she was making a good living as a musician, singing her own songs for appreciative audiences in Lahaina.

Alicia is some kind of fairy godmother, a '60s hippie who never did grow up or bend to the pressure to go straight, get a job, drive a BMW. Maui is the kind of place where you can ignore the demands of the constipated world if you want to. You can believe in magic, and it's all around. The unreconstructed freaks, leftovers from the Summer of Love who never made the transition to the Me Decade, are still around and clustered in "power spots" like Big Sur, Santa Cruz, and Maui, beautiful places where living is laid back.

The great poet W. S. Merwin was one of our neighbors,

living next door to the Maui Zendo where the roshi led students in daily sitting meditations. Kawaharada's Restaurant in Haiku made the finest pies in the world but ran out of them by noon daily. If you didn't get there early, you didn't get pie and the place closed its doors when the last piece was gone. Anywhere else on earth, they'd bake more pie to meet popular demand, but on Maui they'd rather have the afternoon off. The same kind of thinking pervaded the Maui Potato Chip Company, makers of those indescribably delicious Kitch'n Cooked chips. Tourists on airplanes bring them back to America in carry-on shopping bags, but the company, despite repeated opportunities, has refused to expand to the mainland or increase its output of these unique snacks. You can't even get Maui chips in Honolulu. But their widespread fame created a pseudo-Hawaiian chip industry on the mainland, and you can find "Hawaiian-*style*" chips everywhere.

For sheer natural beauty it's hard to beat Maui. Every day of the year some outstanding scenic impression, powerful weather, or other natural phenomenon left us breathless. The bumpy road to Hana was an exploration beyond beauty into ecstacy. Plant life and birds are more colorful than anywhere else on earth, and at the outskirts of Hana you can check into the Waianapanapa State Park, ancient burial cliffs of the Polynesian kings, and—with advance reservations—rent a rustic cabin at camping rates. The expensive hotels on Kaanapali Beach don't want you to know it, but state parks in Hawaii offer dirt-cheap accommodations in paradisiacal surroundings. You have to plan ahead and there's no cocktail bar with wicky-wacky tropical drinks at seven bucks a pop, but you'll find the soul of the islands.

There aren't many directions to go on Maui. If you're not driving on the island coast road on the way to Hana or the other direction, to the gleaming hotels on the dry side, then you have to go straight up. The Haleakala volcano rises in the middle, and you can drive right up to the crater and walk in, to a moonscape of sword lilies and weird vibrations. Some said that aliens from outer space landed in the Haleakala crater, and who could doubt it? Friends urged us to join them camping up there, but after experiencing the eruption of Mount Saint Helens in Washington state from a campground only fifty miles away, I was in no mood to sleep in a volcano.

Halfway up the mountain, in the almost unbelievably pretty village of Kula ("it's coolah in Kula"), lives a man who really was a cultural force in the 1960s and really found a way to make a living on Maui without disturbing his ideals. David Kapralik had been a successful record producer at CBS in Los Angeles, producing some of the most popular artists of the time. When he retired young with a bundle of money ("I got re-tired, and with my new tires I'm rolling again!") he adopted the stage name Ilili and launched himself into a musical career. Ilili and his faithful sidekick Hymie performed New Age songs and skits with stringed instruments, clown face, and zany Renaissance costumes and entertained children, senior citizens, fair-goers, library patrons, street people, any audience they could find. They put out a cassette tape and were reviewed in *New Age Journal*.

But the Ilili and Hymie show never really made any money. It was essentially financed by David's record industry residuals. Eventually the pair split up, Hymie stayed in L.A., and Ilili moved to Maui, where he established Ili Ili farms in Kula, growing and shipping Maui protea, outrageous flowers, and Maui sweet onions, delectable vegetables, around the world. David Kapralik found himself standing in a field overlooking the curving coastline and beaches and the infinite blue Pacific as far as the horizon and declared it home.

His house is a lovely munchkin home, redolent of aromatic flowers and herbs, and he maintains a private restaurant—the Mustard Seed—in a screened patio perched on top of the world. Eating dinner there, watching the sunset ignite the ocean, was like tiptoeing around God's kitchen.

The Pukulani Highway, Makawa, Puunene, these are places lost in space and time, farther from "civilization" than the relatively few miles separating them from airport, hotels, rental cars, and plastic leis. You go live in the back-roads of Maui, you might never be found again. Our Zen friends showed us to many secret waterfalls, tiny cabins far from electric lines or paved roads, sacred places where only the natives go and no Westin Resort chain has arrived. Yet.

Broke in paradise, we were nonetheless the envy of all our friends on the mainland, and more than once our house-guests visiting from California or New York actually paid the rent or bought groceries. It was still a good deal cheaper for them than paying for a hotel room and restaurant meals, and everybody benefited.

Old pal Bob Norris turned up one day, fresh from nine months of cooking for hundreds of men at a mining camp in Wyoming. Norris was a novelist and free spirit who sup-ported himself doing odd jobs, mostly short-order cooking, in order to maintain a vagabond lifestyle and time enough to write. He arrived on Maui with thousands of dollars in savings, no commitments, no desire to ever go back to Amer-ica, and a wild urge to party all night with wine, women, and ritual psychedelics.

He moved into our guest bedroom, paid the rent, brought home cases of cold beer, threw good money after bad into a piss-poor Volkswagen, wrote his novels like a fiend all day, and wondered where to go from Haiku, Maui. It was already clear that Robear and I had burned out on the tropical fantasy and would take the first available plane ticket back to California. We sat around with Norris every night, eating homemade banana bread and cocktails made with cheap vodka and backyard passion fruit, and talked about all the places we'd been. For some reason, Norris wanted to hear more about Japan. It seemed to offer him something the U.S. did not, simply a way to make a living (teaching English) in a dignified, white-collar fashion in-stead of slinging hash and flipping eggs in a greasy kitchen.

Finally the inevitable happened. My boyfriend got a job offer back in Monterey, as marketing director for a burgeon-ing young software corporation, and our time on da island was over. We left the Deardens' house to Norris, who lived there another month or so before splitting to Japan and leaving the place under the care of some itinerant freaks associated with the Zendo. We later heard that burglars came, sensitive perhaps to the abandoned nature of the place, and made off with the color television set and other valuables. I felt bad, and still do, and miss that grass shack, those amazing sunsets, and that life of eternal repose. We totally renovated the house, painting every surface from floor to ceiling, and tilled the garden bursting with blooms, but our visa to paradise simply expired.

Norris went on to Japan on a one-way ticket and his last hundred dollars, promptly got hired to teach, married Shi-chan, and started rooting for the Hankyu Braves.

BOOK II
WRITERS' JAMBOREE

Chapter 8
Creative States Quarterly

CHRISTMAS EVE OF 1982, we got off the plane from Maui and breathed California air again. It felt *cold* but good to be back on the mainland, in a territorial America that doesn't extend to small islands in the deep blue South Pacific.

What chiefly lured us back was a job at an emerging small company called Lifetree Software, Inc., makers of the word-processing program Volkswriter. Lifetree was the quintessence of a baby boomer enterprise. Its president, founder, author, and general big cheese was Camilo Wilson, a native Chilean in his early thirties who had moved to the U.S. with his family as a teenager.

This bespectacled young entrepreneur became a devotee of guru Oscar Ichazo and a member of the New Age mind-control Arica Institute, through which he met and fell in love with Honey Williams, a former SDS official and confidante of California Governor Jerry "Moonbeam" Brown. They settled on the Monterey Peninsula, and Camilo wrote Volkswriter for the IBM personal computer and clones, at a time when word processors were new on the market.

Camilo and Honey surrounded themselves and Lifetree

with other people their own age, mostly in their twenties and thirties, and the company went boldly forward into the software marketplace from an amateur base, starting in a one-room office way out in rural Carmel Valley. In short, nobody knew from experience how to conduct the business (the office manager was an eighteen-year-old boy wonder computer hacker) and all *kinds* of chaos descended. Yet Lifetree succeeded in spite of mistakes, confusions, near-bankruptcies, and the agonies of keeping creative, eccentric people on the staff.

Volkswriter captured an early share of the market because it was (and is) genuinely easy to learn and use, "the people's word processor," if you will. Relative to others, it was also cheap, or "low end" in industry lingo. The German-ness of the name offended some people, those who would never buy a Volkswagen car or any other German product, but of course Volkswriter was not only completely American but completely Californian. "It's not just user-friendly, it's user-*amorous*," wrote Anne Germain in the *Monterey Herald*.

The one-room office in Carmel Valley progressed to a suite in downtown Monterey, then an entire floor of a brand-new office building in the shadow of the gleaming, high-rise Monterey Sheraton. Every recycled movement freak in town seemed to be working at Lifetree, myself included. I wrote ads, brochures, newsletters, and company poetry (yes) and shipped Volkswriters all over the world as part of a zany call-in shipping crew made up of international adventurers like myself, Jean Baptiste Merlin from Paris, and John Miller from Shropshire, England.

One Lifetree tradition in the early years was the daily "train" to the rooftop of the building, where we smoked joints and enjoyed the scenic ocean and mountain views. "Train's coming down the track," one employee or another chanted, and people drifted away from their desks, one by one, until a small crowd formed on the roof. Once I even broadcast a message over the company intercom phone system, heard throughout the firm: "Train's arriving at the station in five minutes, everyone!"

(Of course the trains don't run at Lifetree Software any more. If they did, I wouldn't be writing about it. This kind of frivolity may be possible in a small, friendly enterprise, but as the company grew and grew, it developed more rules and inhibitions. By the time it had fifty employees, Lifetree even needed a personnel policies manual, which I authored.)

Another fine tradition that lasted for years but is now gone forever was the Friday afternoon party. That is, *every* Friday afternoon, without exception, the entire company knocked off work around 3 P.M. and gathered for a party including full, complimentary bar and extravagant hors d'oeuvres. The parties were held in various parts of the business offices, or occasionally in the outdoor courtyard, or at one of the expensive Monterey restaurants. Camilo Wilson treated the Friday party as a goodwill gesture to his employees, as well as a chance for all of them to interact and talk shop about the week's production and the following week's goals.

This approach was no doubt part of the "human resources management" Camilo had learned at the Arica Institute. I've never been too fond of those kinds of programs, including est and Lifespring, quasipsychological approaches to helping people realize their inner potential. There always seems to be a wide latitude for doublespeak and pop-psych gobbledygook, and they always charge a fortune for seminars and workshops led by speakers with unconventional credentials. However, the Friday party was a brilliant PR stroke for Lifetree Software. One's friends couldn't quite believe that a serious employer hosted its entire staff to a lavish party—sometimes including caviar, clams on the half shell, jumbo prawns, sushi, steak tartare, roast beef, premium liquors on call, and *je ne sais quoi* and sometimes, not too often, speeches by company bigwigs—every single week. It was too good to be true, and prospective employees lined up for jobs.

Of course, it was also too good to last, but it went on for years. The flip side of the coin, the misery, was the high stress and extreme capriciousness of the software industry in general and Lifetree in particular. There was always some grave drama being played out, people being fired, people resigning in protest, people working three days and nights without rest on some overdue deadline and burning out.

In the software trade, you have to continually develop and bring out new products that make your old products obsolete. A word-processing program on a computer diskette is like a phonograph record or tape in that it can be easily and cheaply copied. While Volkswriter sold for $100 to $300 (depending on the model and on where you bought it), it could be copied onto blank diskettes or a hard disk for practically nothing. Therefore the company had to produce Volkswriter 2, Volkswriter 3, Volkswriter 4, and so forth, with each new edition incorporating valuable features not previously available. Existing, registered Lifetree users were allowed to purchase an upgrade to the latest level of Volkswriter for a fraction of the new price.

Trouble was, in the mad rush to bring out new editions of its product, Lifetree advertised and sold the upgrades before they were completed and ready to ship. As back orders built up, tempers rose, and stress pushed the employees to outer limits. The worst job of all was the receptionist's; poor Kathleen Kettmann, who had distinguished herself working for Jerry Brown and had managed the great American Peace Walk, was reduced to answering phone calls from irate software buyers. Some of them were referred to the shipping department, where we invented a fictitious Chuck Armstrong as manager. "Chuck" would reassure the frustrated customer that his new Volkswriter would be shipped promptly, then forget all about it.

By the third edition of Volkswriter, Lifetree included a sophisticated spelling checker, for which I researched the correct spelling of more than seventy-five thousand words. It might sound like a dreary assignment, but it was more fun than work for one who *likes* words. However, don't let the computer ads convince you that any spelling checker is perfect. They are highly susceptible to error. The English language is fiendishly complex, and the rules of spelling are full of exceptions. (The machine could never distinguish *there* from *they're* or *soul* from *sole*, for example, and when it came to proper nouns such as a person's name, it was about useless.)

The software business in general went soft after the first few years in which it seemed to grow wildly, without limits. Like most others, Robear and I left Lifetree Software burned out from all the stress (and maybe all that exposure to VDT radiation and high technology), but the business provided us with some handsome paychecks while it lasted, a stable underpinning for our new lives in California. Pulling away from the Volkswriter fountain of dollars, we determined to go into business for ourselves. Some absolute madness, some temporary insanity, persuaded us to launch a magazine.

"A magazine? You've got to be out of your minds," friends told us, friends who had themselves launched and buried magazines after agonizing years of profitless labors. And it wasn't as though I hadn't had the same experience myself, more than once. Liberation News Service catered to small newspapers and magazines and led directly to our publishing a small magazine from the LNS farm, *Green Mountain Post*. We made grocery and cigarette money selling it for fifty cents a copy on street corners in Boston and New York. It lasted six or eight issues and published great stuff by all of our crowd—fiction, poetry, offbeat nonfiction, cartoons, letters, photos—but it never really supported anyone or paid the rent.

Paul Williams, who had succeeded in founding *Crawdaddy*, the rock and roll magazine, nonetheless managed only one issue of his *Rallying Point* magazine before folding. *Ramparts* folded in San Francisco. Even *Life* and *Look* and the *Saturday Evening Post* went under, so what made us think we could make money publishing another magazine?

Sheer self-delusion, no doubt. While staying at James Herlihy's place in L.A., Robear had designed an engagement calendar called the *Creative Planner*. It incorporated the best art and writing we could gather from our friends, including Kurt Vonnegut and Tom Robbins, into a daybook format with space to write in appointments. We took a splendid prototype calendar to the American Booksellers Association convention in 1982, but the production costs frightened off most publishers. We finally sold the design by an oral agreement with Bo Tree Publishers in northern California, but in the end they too backed off the project. We were then left with a gorgeous but unpublishable calendar and a healthy inventory of great visuals and writing, with signed permissions giving us broad rights to use the material.

Why not, we reasoned, publish a small—OK, *literary* (dreaded stamp of poverty)— magazine and bring this wonderful stuff to the world in a form we could afford?

Why not? Because nobody in recent history has made a profit publishing a literary magazine, that's why not. To compensate for that unfortunate fact, we decided to incorporate as a nonprofit, educational, tax-exempt company dedicated to promoting the literary arts and literacy in California as well as publishing the new *Creative States Quarterly*. That way, we could legally qualify for grants and awards, and people could contribute money to our cause and get a tax deduction! Elementary!

We launched *Creative States* with the tried-and-true Lifetree approach, offering subscriptions by mail order long before we had a finished magazine off the press. Robear's mother, Barbara Yamaguchi, herself an artist and a tireless organizer of nonprofit arts events and benefits in L.A., single-handedly sold a couple of hundred subscriptions. We invented another fictitious person, an advertising manager called Mike Squires (no relation to the actual Mike Squires, a former utility infielder with the Chicago White Sox) who, miraculously, got ads from Jockey shorts, Bose sound speakers, major New York publishers, and a mail-order men's clothing supplier.

Incredibly, the premier edition of *Creative States* appeared to have more than paid for itself by the time it came off the press. Then again, perhaps not so incredibly, since we had sold subscriptions for six issues and spent all the money producing the first. We still owed five more issues to virtually all the people we knew in the world.

Our New York editor, Michael Golden, submitted a questionnaire to a number of writers, asking for their replies to such pithy questions as "If you died right now, what would you want on your tombstone?" and "When you lose your sense of humor, where do you find it?" We ran a selection of the answers as a "Writers' Jamboree Questionnaire" with contributions from Ken Kesey, Robert Anton Wilson, Tuli Kupferberg, Seymour Krim, Sally Detroit, Andrei Codrescu, Ann Chandonnet, and many others.

Asked "What do you want on your tombstone?" B. Prune wrote, "Be Right Back." Seymour Krim preferred "He stuck to jazz good cheer through thick n' thin, occasionally with a rainbox sax." Welch Everman reported he "lost my sense of humor when Ford pardoned Nixon. Recently, I regained it watching a rerun of *Knute Rockne—All American.*"

Included were gems here and there:

Does an artist have a responsibility to the society he or she lives in, even if that society is not receptive to what he or she does? If so, what? And how do or don't you live up to it?

"The artist has a responsibility to the truth. A culture which ignores, suppresses, persecutes or expels its artists doesn't want to look at itself too closely & will only tolerate art which serves its ideology, either with propaganda or triviality. Art which ignores, suppresses, persecutes or expels truth will be forgotten."—Ingrid Swanberg

With all the different scenarios possible for this planet, what do you see?

"We will see more revolutionary changes in the next 10-20 years than in ALL previous history. We will *either* blow up *or* establish a new level of energy-wealth worldwide, which will make it increasingly unlikely that we will ever blow up. That is, the technology which makes it possible to blow up everybody on the planet 1,700 times *also* makes it

possible to make everybody a millionaire. I think Bucky
Fuller is right—it is either Utopia or Oblivion, by 1999."
—Robert Anton Wilson

Describe this energy called God.
"Look in the mirror and watch the clown."—Merritt
Clifton

What's the biggest lie that's been perpetrated on us?
"Honesty pays."—Sally Detroit

Name the seven basic plots.
"There are five. The second and fifth and the fourth
and seventh are really the same."—Chick Terlitzky

*With the state of the world so obviously out of control, how
do you go about planning for the future?*
"The world is never out of control, and we do not plan
the future. We merely guess."—Ken Kesey

What one question makes you most uncomfortable?
"Why do you want this job?"—Ligi

What's your favorite fantasy?
"Paris."—Andrei Codrescu

Included also were an "interview" with Tom Robbins,
actually patched-together comments from Robbins at various times and from his letters with a snippet from his new
novel *Jitterbug Perfume* and an original poem about ten-pin
bowling called "Homage to the Chinese Master, Bo-ling,"
and an original watercolor picture by Kurt Vonnegut, from
his New York exhibition, together with comments about
Vonnegut from other leading authors.

These plaudits to Kurt were collected in a limited edition festschrift book, five hundred copies cloth-bound and
in a slipcase, called *Happy Birthday Kurt Vonnegut* and
published by Dell on his sixtieth birthday. Norman Mailer,
Jerzy Kosinski, John Leonard, George Plimpton, Garry
Trudeau, and Tom Wicker all contributed warm essays (as
did I), but my favorite in the collection was John Updike's
"Sonnet on Kurt's Sixtieth":

Kurt Vonnegut, my shelfmate, have you noticed
that not only Leon Uris comes between us

but Gore Vidal? There are too many writers.
One of the reasons we—we, the people—love you
is: you give us gifts of silence, silence
in the spaces between your short paragraphs,
in the times between your rather short novels,
and in the wise unwisdom of "So it goes."

You have a wonderful Midwestern voice
taking pains to be clear, and the bloodshot eyes
of a beagle who has found a cozy place between
the rails of a fireside rocking chair.
Don't wag your tail. Don't smoke too much. Don't stop
giving us news from space, O Festschriftmann.

Vonnegut has been an avuncular, comforting presence in my galaxy of friends. He is a good friend indeed and really seems to care about other writers. I have been with him on the beach at Barnstable, Massachusetts, where he lived before he got rich, and in the town house on New York's East Side, where he is husband to photographer Jill Krementz and daddy to their young daughter. We once shared an endless elevator ride with two creepy critics who berated him from the twelfth to the fortieth floor, but he is a giant, stands tall, shrugs off the "literary establishment" mentality that doesn't take his books seriously. His readers don't care; they eagerly devour each new volume.

Kurt actually saved my life once, although he didn't realize it, by inviting me out to dinner with Jill and himself at a tony French restaurant, following a New York memorial service for William Saroyan.

When his invitation came, I was in my third day without food, living in a borrowed Greenwich Village apartment in sweltering August. Friends and sympathetic editors had all left town on vacation, and I was reduced to living on New York City tap water. Kurt called, and I raced over to the funeral, sat through Vonnegut's speech and other tributes to the great Saroyan, entered the restaurant with Kurt and Jill, and within sixty seconds had devoured ALL the French bread sitting in a basket on the table. Without batting a lash,

Vonnegut summoned the waiter to bring another basket and offered me a Pall Mall to pass the time waiting. "Did you know," he said, "that the Authors Guild keeps a special fund for emergency loans to authors in need?" He then told me who to contact.

Also gracing our premier issue were the author of *Famous All Over Town*, Danny Santiago, with a short story about an East Coast squirrel transplanted to the L.A. Zoo who dies of heartbreak waiting for winter to arrive; Bob Armstrong, with zany Couch Potato Comix; travel writer John Krich on Calcutta, excerpted from his new book *Music in Every Room: Around the World in a Bad Mood*; the Reverend Ivan Stang, mad perpetrator of the Church of the Sub-Genius, on "My Day in Traffic Court"; Dave Sterritt on why movies stink; Aaron Paley, director of the L.A. Fringe Festival, on the last carhop in L.A.; "Chef Robaire" on international cooking; and poet Verandah Porche on the Red Sox.

A pretty good lineup, we thought, although we took some heat for not having more women contributors and in subsequent issues observed a policy of gender equality. We even created controversy in our second issue with a carefully researched piece that credited Carol Henning Steinbeck (John Steinbeck's first wife) with much of the writing of *Grapes of Wrath* and *Tortilla Flats*.

"Carol felt free to change not only words and phrases, but whole paragraphs," biographer Gene Detro effectively proved. Steinbeck, however, was both a misogynist and a philanderer and hated giving credit for his inspiration to a woman, although the dedication to *Grapes of Wrath* says that Carol "willed" the book. *San Francisco Chronicle* columnist Herb Caen's reaction was, "The Steinbeck piece belongs in the annals of history. It has the ring of truth and the stamp of authenticity."

Barbara Yamaguchi, *Creative States*'s single most enthusiastic supporter, died September 1, 1985, and our third issue featured one of her *Other Garden* paintings in brilliant color (our first glossy cover) and this poem from the award-winning poet and children's author Norma Farber, who also had recently passed away.

A Prosody

Unless you have to begin
a sentence with it, death
is only a lower-case noun,
five-letter word at that,
longer than life, love
or terser call of need,
even than loss, void,
almost long enough
to qualify for breath
with which it rhymes and (not
exactly) slantly, health

Barbara was only sixty and in apparently fine health; her death was one of life's sudden thunderclaps, leaving us in a state of shock. What seemed like a thousand people filled the cavernous Los Angeles funeral parlor for the memorial service. All of her friends from the theater guild and art galleries she supported turned out, and she was eulogized as one who loved life, art, and truth. She was outspoken, un-conventional, generous, talented, eccentric, and wise. She was our "red-hot Mama Yama."

Publishing the magazine without her was a depressing prospect, but we published it in her memory, you might say. By the fourth issue we decided to do a "Writers' Jamboree Special" since the famous "Writers' Jamboree Question-naire" had been the most popular thing *Creative States* ever published. And in planning such a special issue, we con-ceived the notion of throwing an *actual* Writers' Jamboree to coincide with the appearance of the magazine.

But we didn't know what we meant by the term. A jamboree is a large gathering of Boy Scouts in conventional slang. The Oxford dictionary, however, defines jamboree as "celebration, merry-making (19th cent., unknown orig.)." The word was picked up, but not invented by, the scouts. Our Writers' Jamboree, then, would be a gathering of writ-ers for a merry celebration, a big party for the literary set, not a stuffy conference or academic affair but something wild and out of control, something dangerous.

Chapter 9
Jambo to the Max

GEORGE FULLER was the editor of *Monterey Life* magazine, a slick monthly magazine that existed mostly to tout the virtues of the Monterey Peninsula to tourists. It was given away in hotel rooms, but not many local people read *Monterey Life*, at least not until Fuller came aboard in 1986 and breathed new life into it with fresh, relevant articles. George was thirtyish, hip, friendly and operated the magazine like a personal vehicle and a social club for writers. It became a pleasure to drop in and hang around the offices.

George is also a poet and publisher of the *Santa Cruz Poet* series of paperbacks, so he was that rarest of things, an editor who is also a writer and advocate of writers' concerns. From his description of it, he got the job editing *Monterey Life* just because he happened to be standing there, freelance submission in hand, the day the previous editor was fired. He was one of the leading spirits of the National Writers Union local chapter number seven. And he was more than delighted to help us stage the first Writers' Jamboree.

With the help of *Monterey Herald* reporter Al Goodman, and quite a few Stolichnaya Bloody Marys from the bar at the Clock Garden restaurant in Monterey, George happily joined Robear and me and *Creative States* in planning this extravaganza for Saturday, November 22, 1986. He offered the *Monterey Life* offices, atop José's Fine Mexican restaurant, as a locale for afternoon seminars, while the Thunderbird Bookshop in Carmel agreed to host an evening party in its restaurant and patio, which could hold about two hundred people.

It's worth noting that the Thunderbird, Carmel's leading bookstore, had established a precedent to the Writers' Jamboree some years earlier, called the Grand Authors Assembly, and had abandoned doing it. The concept of the GAA was a gathering of all the authors who reside in the Monterey/Carmel/Big Sur coastal area; these writers enjoyed a social hour to themselves, then the general public was admitted at five dollars a ticket to mingle with the authors and purchase autographed books from them.

You cannot *imagine* the problems this Grand Authors Assembly arrangement created. Since no standards were enforced, anyone who had self-published a book, or had had one published by a small press, or had had a book published once a long time ago qualified as a resident author entitled to a free ticket, food, and wine. Soon the "grand author" list included a woman whose only writing output was religious verse published in Tennessee twenty years earlier, lots of poets who published their own stuff, etc.

Every one of these "authors" had to receive his own personal name tag and the bookstore had to stock his book, or take a few copies on consignment, so that the author could sign and sell books to the public at the event. With the exception of a few legitimate bestselling authors in the community, most of these writers and their books had zero sales appeal. The paperwork involved in keeping track of all this was a nightmare, and any author who was overlooked, or whose book didn't make it, or whose name tag was not ready, was entitled to an ego fit. Worse yet, the *real* writers began to boycott the event so as not to be associated with the amateurs.

Finally, of course, the authors outnumbered the general public willing to pay five dollars to meet them. The event, meant as a benefit to raise funds for a local school library, actually lost money. You find that authors can drink quite a lot of wine if it's free and nobody's asking for an autograph.

The Writers' Jamboree concept was different in all respects. We couldn't afford to offer free tickets to writers simply because they were local residents, but we did institute "scholarship" tickets for authors in need. We didn't even *try* to sell books except those of our guest speakers, although plenty of writers brought copies of their own books to sell, trade, show, tell, sign, or give away. We added educational seminars in the daytime to give the event solid value to the local writing community and made the evening party completely open to everyone, whether writer, reader, or illiterate.

We quickly put together some excellent panel speakers from San Francisco and L.A.. The first of two seminars, "Writing for Love and Money," featured editors Bernard Ohanian from *Mother Jones* magazine, Amy Rennert of *San Francisco Focus*, and Fuller, plus author Mark Dowie from the Center for Investigative Reporting and *Monterey Herald* writer Goodman, talking about how to sell freelance articles and stories to periodicals. The second seminar was "Lit Biz 101, the Business of Literature," and featured William Webb, a national publishers' representative; Robert Sheldon, president of Trade Book Marketing in Berkeley; and myself, talking about book publishing. Both seminars included a lot of questions and answers from the audience.

Bestselling author Jessica Mitford, best known for her landmark book *The American Way of Death*, graciously agreed to be our special guest star. I was worried about how we could possibly accommodate a half dozen out-of-town guest speakers until George showed me the simple business of comping hotel rooms. We could get free hotel rooms, he said, if we simply provided the hotels with some free publicity in return! It seemed too easy, but *Monterey Life* was the leading tourist publication in the area, and I marveled at the smoothness with which George called up public relations directors and manipulated the comps, including a hospitality suite for the Writers' Jamboree insiders in the brand-new Monterey Plaza Hotel on the Cannery Row waterfront, made famous by Steinbeck.

Once we got started on this road to ruin, nothing would stop us. We called the PR director of the Monterey Vineyard and found he was happy to donate cases of his best wine and gift packs of wine and corkscrews bearing his corporate logo for our visiting journalists from the *Los Angeles Times* to the *Carmel Pine Cone*. Shayna Selby, a member of our board of directors and daughter of a major Dallas liquor distributor, used her connections to produce free cases of superb "boutique" wines from smaller California wineries. *Monterey Life* put up typesetting, copying, long-distance phone calls, and massive amounts of stationery supplies in addition to the seminar rooms. Lloyd Morain, editor of *The Humanist* magazine, showed up with a major cash contribution. Lifetree Software became the official word processor of the Writers' Jamboree, with free computers and services. We were showered with generosity from the community.

The night before the Jambo was to take place, all of the perpetrators gathered in our hospitality suite at the Plaza, outfitted with a complete bar, vast quantities of donated wine, hors d'oeuvres, and recreational drugs. The buzz level was something to marvel at, as writers and editors streamed into town from up and down the West Coast. A vast rumor mill manipulated by George and the *Creative States* staff publicized the Jambo far and wide; a kind of call went out, saying, *"Party time for writers on the Monterey Peninsula!"*

One of our guest speakers, a *Los Angeles Times* investigative reporter I'll call Tim Jones, failed to show up. We had already reserved a free room for him in the hotel, and George wanted to use it himself so he could continue partying all night and not have to drive fifty miles to his home in Santa Cruz. The question became how to pass George off as Tim Jones from the *Los Angeles Times* when the hotel staff knew him quite well as the editor of the local *Monterey Life*.

We needed a volunteer willing to pretend to be Jones, and I somehow got the job by default. Everybody else was too chicken.

Convulsive with laughter and chanting "You're Jones now, you're Jones now," the happy throng sent us off from the hospitality suite to the lobby, until someone noticed that I was barefoot. We found my shoes and managed to keep straight faces just long enough for "Jones" to check in and get all his keys and polite greetings. The hotel staff shook my hand and warmly welcomed me as representing the *Los Angeles Times*, then George and I raced to the elevators before erupting into uncontrollable giggling.

The party went on all night.

Saturday dawned, and we set up fifty folding chairs in the office to accommodate the anticipated crowd. Only about thirty people had purchased tickets in advance, but we expected *some* walk-up business at the box office. We were unprepared, however, for the *avalanche* that followed. Writers were lined up around the block waiting to get in. We squeezed every single body into the modest-sized room and brought up all the portable chairs from José's Fine Mexican Restaurant. The elderly and handicapped were seated first, while others sat on desktops, window sills, bookshelves, stools, cartons of magazines, and a folding card table. It was stultifyingly hot, which required us to open the windows and admit a breeze along with all the traffic noise from the street below. But nobody complained, and participants hung on every word from our panels. From the transcripts:

Mark Dowie, investigative reporter: "One of the ways to operate as a writer is to collaborate with your editor and to form up front a strong collaborative bond with your editor. Make it clear to your editor that you want to work with him. The other thing I noticed about when I was and wasn't successful as a journalist is that I was more successful selling myself as a technician than selling a story idea. If you're going to be a professional magazine writer, people have to know you're going to do a good job on a story, not just that you have a good idea for one. Editors are conceited too, and they sit around thinking up story ideas and then say, 'Who can we get to write it?' "

Amy Rennert, editor of San Francisco Focus: "A good place to get into the book if you haven't been published before is not necessarily with a big feature idea but with a short piece. I think that's true of most city and national books. [*Book* is a common trade word for magazine.] What really matters to me in meeting writers is not only a specialty interest but having a real passion for a certain story. If someone comes in who is really passionate about the story and also has the skills as a writer, I'm more likely to be interested."

Bernard Ohanian, editor of Mother Jones *magazine:* "My first rule of thumb is that you have to convince the editor that you are going to do a thorough job on the story. But as an editor, what fires me up is when the writer can convince me the story is really worth caring about. The details are easier filled in. We get forty to fifty query letters a week, and we might consider publishing two or three articles out of them. The successful ones are written cogently and passionately. Articles sort of find their own length. Unfortunately, most pieces of nine thousand words are better at three or four thousand."

George Fuller, editor of Monterey Life *magazine:* "There may be twenty thousand magazines in the country, and I'll bet that any well-written story can be sold. Find something unique, and it will fly. I use a lot of manuscripts from cold queries in the mail."

Robert Sheldon, president of Trade Book Marketing, Berkeley: "Begin with the literary contract. You can write certain guarantees into the contract or original agreement allowing you to share the responsibility for promoting the book. Then work with the rep in your area. Do autograph signings, etc. If your book is positioned near the top of the publisher's list, you're more than likely to find the publisher happy to have your cooperation. But if it's four months after publication, don't expect anything to happen. It's too late."

William Webb, publishers' representative: "An editor at

McGraw-Hill told me, 'We get seventeen thousand unsolicited manuscripts a year and only one percent of it is publishable. How can any publisher handle it?' Ask yourself the question. There's no way. On the one hand, publishers are desperate for good books to publish, and on the other hand they are besieged by useless, bad, inconsequential material."

After all that heady material and four hours of questions and answers between audience and panels, some two hundred people repaired to the Thunderbird Bookshop for wine, food, and hearty partying. "Writers Gather for Rip-Roaring Event," the *Monterey Herald* coverage was headlined. Guest author Jessica Mitford signed what seemed like a thousand copies of *The American Way of Death*. An impromptu jazz trio made up entirely of published authors played music for dancing and inebriated singing of "All of Me" and other standards. *Herald* editor Anne Germain escorted Miss Mitford back to the Monterey Plaza and our hospitality suite, only to find it in disarray, with the couch opened as a bed and the bedsheets tossed about, obviously used, empty wine bottles rolling around the floor, and so forth.

When the bookshop finally kicked out the revelers around 11 P.M., the most hard-core partyers, maybe seventy-five to one hundred of them, moved the bash over to the hotel, where it raged on a second night till dawn. A couple of refugees from the Hooker's Ball in San Francisco turned up. The hotel was forced to move all the guests in our wing to new rooms farther from the deafening racket. "There was dancing on the tables, and that sort of thing," Germain reported daintily.

Better yet, when the dust had cleared and all bills were paid, the Writers' Jamboree showed a modest return, not to say "profit" since it was and is a nonprofit event. There was enough money left over to pay every speaker a tiny honorarium, with a small reserve set aside to publicize the next Writers' Jamboree, which we scheduled for the vernal equinox, March 21, 1987.

The very idea of making money, no matter how little, while having so much fun, was *obscene*. We loved it. Despite portents of trouble and strife from syndicated astrologer Sydney Omarr, we couldn't wait to Jambo twice.

"Suddenly it's spring," wrote Anne Germain in the *Monterey Herald* after our March 21, 1987, second Jamboree. "Naturally we expected serene sunshine and blossoms for the first day of spring, but what we got was no surprise to astrologer Sydney Omarr, who charted a 'personal horoscope' for the Writers' Jamboree:

" 'It will exude an aura of excitement and danger,' he wrote. 'It will be anything but dull . . . both horrible and wonderful. . . . The participants will be carrying the proverbial smoking gun.' "

Well, Omarr wasn't wrong. A novelist published by Henry Holt and Company assaulted the stage, raining verbal abuse on the book review editor of a major West Coast newspaper; nineteen women members of the National Writers Union staged a protest over what they considered a scandalous imbalance in speakers (eighteen men and only six women); the lady accompanying a Palm Springs editor was lost overnight and became the object of a police search before turning up the following morning with the writer she'd run off with; the booksellers contracted to handle sales of featured authors' books never paid their bills and disclaimed responsibility for lost cartons of books while the writers howled; the party was disrupted by egotistical temper tantrums, impromptu poetry wars and hot-tempered outbursts, while nature poured thunder, wind, rain, and foul weather on Monterey.

We chose the vernal equinox as the date of the second Jambo in the spirit of rebirth, spring, a traditionally joyous day, but perhaps some planets were warring in the heavens. The event was in trouble from the first. It was to feature four seminars, twice as many as the first Jamboree, with twenty-four speakers including poets reading from their work, a two-night party, and a writers' lunch. It was ambitious and slightly insane, a risky leap in only five months from a bookstore back room to a splashy downtown hotel ballroom.

A small power struggle erupted between *Creative States*, our nonprofit literary foundation, and the local chapter of the National Writers Union, which wanted to use the event to recruit new members. We at *Creative States* carefully disassociated ourselves from any formal relationship with the union chapter, which sold memberships to never-published amateur writers. The union set up a booth and promoted new memberships at the Jamboree, but we made no specific endorsement of it. A palpable tension existed between the two groups, and the Jamboree that had begun as a lark became serious enough for *Creative States* to register a trademark on the term *Writers' Jamboree*. We own the name, so to speak, in the state of California.

While the first event was staged on a minuscule budget of a few hundred dollars, the second Jambo ran thousands into the red as extravagant expenses mounted. Most of our speakers had to be transported from Los Angeles or San Francisco, accommodated at various swank hotels, wined and dined. We even paid a Swiss au pair to babysit infants of several speakers so they could bring their families along to their weekend in Monterey-Carmel. The phone bills and postage expenses and printing costs for promotional literature, programs, and posters soared into the higher realms of finance. We took a chance that the notoriety of the first Jamboree would attract large crowds to the second one; we knew we were risking enormous losses if we failed. The stress level was unendurable. Tempers ran short.

The Monterey Sheraton provided us with a gorgeous hospitality suite adjoining its swimming pool and hot-tub deck. We devoured whole roasts, hams, turkeys, cheeses, sourdough loaves, and other edibles, and the wine flowed copiously as we welcomed speakers and friends the Friday night before the Jambo. We defused the women's protest by proving that we had in fact invited many other women speakers who were unable to make it on that date. We coddled the egos of the assembled authors (and nothing can quite match the level of sheer egotism generated in a roomful of authors), dealt with crises of missing books and tangled air-

port arrangements, and everything seemed to fall into place.
Whew. But would the paying customers materialize, would
we get a good crowd on Saturday?

We did. We nearly filled the Sheraton ballroom all day
long with seminars such as "Desktop Publishing," "Writing
for Love and Money," "Lit Biz 101," and "Getting Your
Novel in Print." Santa Cruz poet Claire Braz-Valentine
opened the day with an invocation, a long prose poem called
"What Is a Writer?" It had people laughing at the realization
of horrible truths:

> *Writers always hang out in stationery stores, book
> stores, and libraries, but mostly they hang out in
> bars. . . .*
> *Writers are known as addictive personalities, either to
> alcohol, caffeine, sex, cigarettes, or writing. The
> best writers are addicted to all of these. . . .*
> *Writers justify every bad thing they ever did by
> rationalizing that it made good writing material
> later. . . .*
> *When writers write, they become most mysterious. When
> the writing is going well, sounds don't bother them.
> When it isn't, the sound of birds shitting in the
> trees in the neighbor's backyard is enough to ruin a
> day's work. . . .*
> *Writers notice tiny details. It's the big things they
> forget. Writers forget the day of the week but they
> can still remember the smell of the candy eggs in
> their first Easter basket as if it was yesterday. . . .*
> *Writers are the chroniclers, the note takers, the
> historians and the proof that we've been here. . . .*
> *They keep our records and these records will be
> called our history.*

The seminars "Desktop Publishing" and "Writing for
Love and Money" played very smoothly before good audiences, while the mezzanine of the hotel was packed with
writers, editors, readers, and fans buying books, chatting,

and exchanging gossip and information. A real networking event was underway. We offered Susan Brenneman, editor of San Francisco's weekly *Image* magazine; Donald George, travel editor of the *San Francisco Examiner*; Walter Bowart, editor of *Guest Life* and *Palm Springs Life*; and Jack Miles, book review editor of the *Los Angeles Times*, among others— all of them editors who "buy freelance," a target market for our local Monterey Peninsula writers. We found, however, after examining our registration forms, that writers had traveled to the Jamboree from all over the state as well as from Oregon, Washington, and even a few from the East Coast.

The poetry reading by the Jazz Press Trio of George Fuller, William Minor, and Robert Sward, scheduled for 1:30 P.M., had to be postponed until evening because the size of the crowds slowed down lunch service. The poets were still waiting for their dessert by the time they were supposed to be onstage. Other than that, however, all went swimmingly until Richard Miller, author of *Snail* and other novels, attacked Jack Miles of the *Los Angeles Times* onstage.

I'm not quite sure what the issue really was, but Miller took objection to much or all that Miles had been saying in the seminar. And he boldly took the stage and railed that the editor was a "total idiot" and many "other unkind sobriquets," as Anne Germain reported. This bit of upstaging was actually good theater, but I doubt that poor Jack Miles appreciated it. He declined to attend the party that followed that evening.

The fourth and last seminar was the most passionate and spirited. "Getting Your Novel in Print" featured four novelists talking about how they came to the profession and how they broke into print. The crowd accorded a standing ovation to Thomas Farber (*Curves of Pursuit*), Robert Gover (*The Hundred Dollar Misunderstanding*), Don Pendleton (*The Executioner* series of thirty-eight paperback novels), and Gerald Rosen (*The Carmen Miranda Memorial Flagpole*). They spun tales of woe and serendipitous luck, for example:

Robert Gover: "I just decided at one point that I had to

quit my job and devote all my time to trying to become a novelist. I came up with *The Hundred Dollar Misunderstanding*. I sent that to my agent, who immediately sent it back saying he hated it. . . . I called up and got his partner and the partner said, 'Send it back, I love it, it's terrific.' He sent the manuscript to an agent in Paris [who] wrote me a letter and said, 'This is a work of art, it's a landmark in literature. I'll get Gallimard to publish it.' . . . Eventually, Ballantine got the American rights, Grove contracted with Ballantine to do the hard cover edition, and when the book appeared the newspapers in New York City went on strike, so all promotion was off. When the lights came on again, the book was number three on the bestseller list by word of mouth. If all the expected promo for other books had been going on, it would probably have never gotten on the bestseller list."

Thomas Farber: "When I started writing I fell into it ass backwards. There was an underground paper in San Francisco called the *Express Times*. . . . I walked into the office one day having just come back from a wedding in Big Sur. I had a friend who worked for the paper, we sat around and I told him the story of the wedding I'd just seen. [Editor] Marvin Garson said, 'You ought to write that down, and I'll publish it,' and I kept writing once Marvin had shown me the way. . . . An editor in New York saw those pieces in this underground paper [and] asked if I'd like to collect them into a book. . . .

"I wrote the book and she published it. It wasn't much of a book, a young man's book, very callow and full of great enthusiasms. Nor did I understand what fiction was. It's a great liberation to get to that distance between what you consider to be the 'truth' and poetic truth. But I worked hard on that book and I learned something, and by the time I'd finished it I was ready to try another. . . .

"You begin with a kind of obduracy, that kind of a flame burning, and you can begin with something as unprepossessing as an underground newspaper in San Francisco."

Don Pendleton: "Don't shrink from the task of getting your stuff marketed. If you don't market it, you might as well

not write it. I don't think any of us would go through the
agony of writing a whole book if we thought no one was ever
going to read it. . . . Keep in mind that you are part of a
money-making industry. Don't try to write like someone
else. Write something you want to share with someone else.
You may then take it to an agent, an editor, even a friend of
a friend, but keep working at it until someone sits down and
reads it and says 'God, I love it.'·"

Gerald Rosen: "The idea of becoming a writer was just
some dream and not for people like me. It was for people in
Manhattan, I always thought, not for people from the
Bronx. I majored in engineering in college, then went to
Wharton Graduate School and got an M.B.A. . . . I got the
idea for my first book when we went to attack the Pentagon
in 1967. Remember that, Norman Mailer wrote about it. I'd
been in the Army and thought, 'I'm one of the few people
who understands both sides of what's going on here. I've
really got a message here.' . . . I wrote a 500-page novel in six
weeks, *Blues for a Dying Nation*. When I finally started
saying what I wanted to say, it just poured out. . . .

"The woman who lived down the street was a friend of
a friend and asked if she could see the manuscript. 'I work
for a publisher,' she said, 'and it would help if I could show
them a book.' I didn't know how to submit it, so I put it in
a metal filing box. They were all laughing as nobody had
ever submitted a book in a metal filing box before. . . .

"I got a call one day and the man said, 'My name is
Robert Gottlieb and I'm the editor in chief of Knopf, we
published *Catch-22*.' He said, 'Joe has your book.' I said,
'Joe?' He said, 'Yes, Joe Heller. We like your book, could you
come in to the office and talk about it?' I said, 'Oh, let me
check my calendar!' "

When these guys finished reminiscing and the floor
opened for questions, one particularly bold person in the
audience posed an interrogatory to all four panelists: "How
many years have you been writing novels, and what's your
net worth?" Don Pendleton, who with thirty-eight novels in
The Executioner series is probably the most prolific of the

group, said, "Let's not get vulgar, but it is possible to get
very wealthy writing books. . . . The trick is to have money
trickling in from a great many sources." Robert Gover said,
"I've been up and down financially. I had a three-book deal
with Pocket Books and thought 'I'm on a roll here, I've got
security.' But my editor's head rolled and instead of 50,000
copies published, they wound up printing 5,000. . . . Last
Thursday I filed chapter 7."

Thomas Farber was brief. "Henry Miller was famous for
his telegrams to friends with the two words, Send Money.
That's my response to net worth: Send Money." Gerald
Rosen added, "I don't think that writing is a good way to
make money. It's much easier to get an M.B.A., really. . . .
But I've had five books published and I must say the money
you make is the sweetest money you ever make, because it
feels like stealing."

Farber added a postscript: "Like Henry Miller, broke in
his forties and a kind of desperado, all real writers are
foolish enough to keep insisting that they are writers and
never give up."

"You'll never get over the psychic scars of doing a thing
like this," chuckled novelist Peter Danielson (pen name of
George Warren), at the unfettered party that followed. Max-
ine Hong Kingston, deep in the throes of writing her mas-
terpiece *Tripmaster Monkey*, came with James and Jeanne
Houston, authors of *Farewell to Manzanar*. Michael Har-
graves, official bibliographer of Henry Miller, drove up
from L.A. Poet Nancy Mairs (*Plaintext*) mingled with nonfiction bestseller Nancy Mayer (*The Male MidLife Crisis*).
Daniel James and Danny Santiago came in one body. The
Sheraton charged money for drinks, a practice decried and
abhorred by all. We got shut down by the cops.

(Well, *technically*. The police didn't actually interrupt
the party, but we were apprehended and interrogated twice
that evening by Monterey and then Pacific Grove police as
we attempted to haul cases of leftover wine from the hotel to
our *Creative States* offices postmidnight. The wine had been

donated and was served free in our hospitality suite; the hotel charged for drinks only at the public party in its lobby, but many authors accustomed to the free booze were irate at being asked to pay two dollars for a drink. We learned from this experience that you can never expect writers to pay for drinks, and you should never drive drunk with a car full of cases of wine and books and a cash box stuffed with thousands of dollars. Alas, we *didn't* learn that one should never throw public parties for authors. Emboldened by success, we carried on, and on, and paid an awful price as you shall see when we continue next chapter. . . .)

Chapter 10
The Summer Solstice–Murder Mansion–Miss Manners Madness

TOM ROBBINS, the great and wildly popular author of novels *Another Roadside Attraction, Even Cowgirls Get the Blues, Still Life with Woodpecker*, and *Jitterbug Perfume*, was a personal friend and contributor to *Creative States* magazine but was unable to join us for the vernal equinox bash. I suggested an alternative date of the summer solstice, June 21, 1987, and he promptly accepted with a note from his Washington state farm:

> Dear Professor Moonglow,
>   If the proposition is the same regarding transportation, accommodations and refreshments, you can count on me absolutely for the summer solstice Jambo. I don't want to deliver a lecture, either formal or informal, but I don't want to just hang around either. I propose that I conduct a Q & A workshop where I would spend two or three or more hours answering any and all questions concerning the practice of fiction and life, death and goofiness. What do you think? The Ship Sails on—.

The very idea of staging another Jambo only three

months after the devastating March 21 event was probably insane, but we had tried three or four earlier times to attract Tom Robbins, and he was always too busy, or writing on deadline, or elsewhere. We reasoned, not incorrectly, that a literary star of his magnitude, an author whose novels regularly land on the national bestseller lists and whose readers number in the millions, would be enough of a roadside attraction to build an entire party around. It didn't seem right to make poor Tom carry the whole show, however, so we paired him in a program with Armistead Maupin, the funny and charming author of *Tales of the City*, *Babycakes*, and *Significant Others*, novels about the yuppie/gay lifestyle of northern California.

Robbins and Maupin were admirers of each others' books but had never met. And Robbins of course is heterosexual, one of the greatest lovers of nubile womanhood indeed, while Maupin is publicly gay. They both exude humor and whimsy, sophistication and joyful sensuality.

We interviewed Armistead Maupin on a balmy Mother's Day in San Francisco, just as he was about to go out on national tour for *Significant Others*. He was joined by his own significant other, Terry Anderson, at Leticia's restaurant, a short walk from the Walt Whitman Bookshop, and their arrival caused an immediate stir, with Sunday brunch patrons straining eagerly for a glimpse of one of San Francisco's most admired writers.

Creative States: The feedback we've gotten from announcing that you and Tom Robbins will appear at the Writers' Jamboree has been wonderful. People are excited about it. You both have cult followings.

> [A toast is raised, and Armistead begins talking about his forthcoming ten-city publicity tour for the new book.]

Armistead Maupin: The trick is to stay fresh on the tour. When *Babycakes* came out in 1984, it was the first time Harper & Row sent me on an extensive tour. They said, 'Are you sure you want to do this? A lot of authors don't like to do it,' and I said, 'But of course I want to do it, this is what I've spent my life trying to make happen.' Then about six days into the tour I heard myself answer the same four questions over and over again and began to get a little disgusted at the sound of my own voice.

CS: It's any good actor's job to make it seem really original even if they've said it a million times before.

AM: Exactly. And you're asked the same four questions because they are the four questions that should be asked.

CS: Does Harper & Row take decent care of you on the road? Do they put you in good hotels?

AM: Yes, they did last time around and I expect they will again. I got lots of complimentary soaps and shampoos.

CS: Wonderful! It matters so much that you can get good rest.

AM: Especially since I spend all of my time in my hotel room when I'm not promoting. There are people who say, 'We want to show you the sights,' but I'm in a work mode and not able to break out of it.

CS: Do you watch TV?

AM: I watch TV. I love "Three's Company." That's the darkest secret I have. There's something so mindless about "Three's Company," I find it comforting.

Waiter: Are you ready to order?

CS: I'll have the eggs benedict, with the shrimp.

Waiter: One benny shrimp.

AM: That's a shrimp on speed. I'll have the regular eggs benedict. This restaurant used to have a transsexual hostess, very beautiful and quite charming. I brought my father here one night with my stepmother, who's a year younger than I am, and my father spent the whole evening flirting with the hostess. At one point he asked her if there were any more like her back home in South Carolina.

CS: How old is your father?

AM: Seventy-four at this point.

CS: Was he aware of her . . . uh . . .?

AM: I told him after that, and curiously he became even more fascinated. He started grabbing her waist and saying 'What a nice firm waist she's got, honey,' making my stepmother wildly jealous.

CS: Does he approve of your lifestyle?

AM: We have a kind of understanding, yes. He sasses me and I sass him.

CS: But you're open about it. . . . You write so well about gays, you must be very well adjusted.

AM: I'm thoroughly convinced that the responsibility lies with gay people to be open about who they are. We cannot expect the world to accept and understand us if we don't communicate.

Terry Anderson: And gay or straight, there are a lot of people who are fucked about their lives. It has nothing to do with their sexuality.

AM: One of the reasons I'm excited about meeting Tom Robbins is that he's a guy who is obviously joyfully comfortable with his sexuality.

TA: I think the world is divided into two segments, people who like sex and those who don't. Sex is a liberator, it really is.

AM: Our worst presidents have been the ones who had no sex lives . . .

CS: *Publishers Weekly* mentioned that you became a spokesman for Rock Hudson after he was diagnosed with AIDS. Is that true?

AM: I was quoted on him. He thought his world was going to come to an abrupt and terrible end when he had that announcement, that he had AIDS. The biggest shock was the fact that 30,000 people wrote and said 'We love you just the way you are.' It was the biggest revelation of his life, really.

CS: Then there's Liberace, who never . . .

AM: Who never felt the joy of knowing that people knew and didn't care! The sadness of that is that he was a deeply homophobic man. Rock, for all his secrecy, was not homophobic. He saw nothing wrong with the way he was. And when he realized that he was going to die and therefore no longer had a career, he said, 'Fuck it, we'll tell the truth.' And he hired a woman to do just that.

CS: Sara Davidson?

AM: Yeah. He gave her a list of his friends to interview. She was just the right person for the job. His friend George Nader, who was the recipient of his estate, turned over his diary to Sara. She called me with some very specific questions. I had to make sure it was really Sara Davidson, because I was afraid it might be the *National Enquirer* or somebody else. People who are gay and happy being gay have to speak up, otherwise homosexuality will always be reported by the scandalmongers. We'll always be the fodder for the *National Enquirer* until we learn to be so forthright that the onus is gone.

CS: Don't you think your audience is a straight one? That is, that you cut across the gay and straight line?

AM: Yes, and there's still a tendency, especially in New York, for journalists to eliminate any mention of my homosexuality in any discussion of my work. A recent piece in *Vanity Fair* didn't mention it at all. They are used to covering up for gay writers.

We left Armistead and Terry after promising them not only a good time with Tom Robbins but a weekend in the seclusion and divine comforts of Big Sur's famous Ventana Inn, personal delivery of the sacred herbs required to appreciate the hot springs, and a speaker's fee.

For Tom Robbins we promised the Highlands Inn, where his pals Timothy Hutton and Debra Winger were spotted honeymooning, and a bevy of female admirers who couldn't wait to tear the clothes off his body.

We designed a dazzling poster reading "Join Tom Robbins and Armistead Maupin on the Summer Solstice" and hand colored each one on fancy parchment paper. The biggest department store in town, Ford's, donated its penthouse restaurant with gorgeous views of the sunset over Monterey

Bay for a three-hour bacchanal of superb hors d'oeuvres,
complimentary Monterey wines, dancing to the music of the
Writers' Jamboree Band, and paying homage to the visiting
authors, who were enthroned in autographing nooks.
Crazed young women appeared, carrying dozens of our
posters for autographing, which explained to us why they'd
been disappearing all over town. A couple of hundred people
had a great time on the longest day of the year, and Robbins
had to be whisked away by Nancy Mayer to escape his adoring fans.

But the event lost money, somehow. A couple of thousand dollars in red ink stained our ledger like blood. We
searched for reasons why we hadn't drawn a bigger crowd. It
was Father's Day and unwise to schedule our event in competition with a major holiday. It *was* a Sunday, with workshop
in the afternoon and party at night—and parties *always* do
better on Saturday night, our faith in astrology notwith-
standing. It *was* too soon after the last Writers' Jamboree
and not really a full-scale Jamboree but rather a celebrity
event.

These rationalizations comforted us, but the bills had
to be paid, and several members of our board of directors
graciously ponied up from their personal funds to bail out
Creative States. The Writers' Jamboree had proven itself
vincible; we learned the hard way that cultural and literary
programs are not necessarily self-supporting. Indeed, most
arts organizations in this country subsist on donations,
corporate sponsors, and the proceeds from benefits. Before
we could do another Jamboree, then, we needed a fundraiser.
Something literary in theme but not educational, something
like a party.

We'd also learned that you can *only* lose money publishing a literary magazine, and we killed *Creative States Quarterly* after six action-packed issues. Our organization would
continue to sponsor programs for writers, but our publication is out of print. It occasionally mutters to be reborn, but
I'm hoping if I ignore the six-foot-tall stack of unsolicited
poetry and short stories that is always growing in my office,
it will *go away*.

The idea came to me in the shower. We had in Carmel the 1987 winner of the Edgar Award for best mystery novel published in the United States, Robert W. Campbell. And we had Ellen Weiner, who owns an original 1918 rock-work mansion on the crashing rocks of the Carmel Highlands coast, on our board of directors. Put these two priceless human resources together, and we could stage one of those murder-mystery parties in an authentic haunted castle!

You know the kind of party I'm talking about. A bunch of actors stage a theatrical murder, and the guests of the party have to figure out who done it. Clues are dropped all over the place and prizes awarded to the guests who solve the mystery. This kind of party usually involves no more than a dozen guests, the playacting and script are amateurish and melodramatic, and nobody takes it too seriously. We decided to do a lavish production for hundreds of guests, with a real script by a serious and acclaimed mystery novelist, a real location in a stone mansion, a cast of the finest veteran performers from local stage companies, a banquet of delectable edibles, a wine bar of unending free flow, a dance band in the ballroom, fabulous prizes including Palm Springs vacations and rooms in luxury hotels, *now how much would you pay?*

Would you pay twenty-five dollars a person including food, wine, play, dancing, castle, and prizes from seven to midnight on a full-moon Saturday night in March? It was to benefit the Writers' Jamboree, a tax-deductible, bona fide *good cause* to boot, and from the beginning we couldn't handle the demand for tickets.

It was fairly easy convincing Bob Campbell to write the plot, although he agreed to provide original characters and a basic story line only. The dialogue was to be improvised or else provided by the director. Of course, we had no director, but I ran into Chuck Thurman, a cofounder of the Monterey Bay Theatre Alliance at a bus stop, and he volunteered for the job instantly. And Ellen Weiner had graciously offered us the use of the castle for a fund-raising benefit, although little aware of the size of the extravaganza we had in mind.

Murder in the Highlands grew like Topsy. Jazz pianist

and author Bill Minor came on board with his ensemble of mellow tunes. Local hotels, restaurants, merchants, and wineries all donated goods and prizes, and our travel agents persuaded a major airline to comp some tickets. The phone started ringing off the hook even before any mention of the party in the newspapers. The director of the Donatello Club in San Francisco, 125 miles away, drove to Carmel with a check for $1,000 to buy fifty tickets for her members, who chartered a bus from the city and booked rooms at the Monterey Plaza. Every television station for miles around petitioned us for permission to take news footage at the party, but the hostess turned them down. Enough was enough, or in this case, too much.

In the early planning we'd all agreed the castle could hold a maximum of two hundred guests. It was a fairly huge stone house, but the individual rooms could be small and we wanted everybody to be able to follow the plot of the mystery. The house would be transformed for one evening into a nightclub—the Magic Mansion by the Sea—owned by the pompous and dangerous Albion Tanner, a tyrannical boss whose employees each had a very good reason to wish him dead. Tanner, played by burly actor Carey Crockett, was to act as host of the party while interacting with the other characters from room to room. Guests could pick up clues by observing the actions and overhearing the dialogue among members of the cast, who were identified with special name tags. They could also ask the cast questions and generally get "into" the play. By 9:30 P.M., we figured to have Albion Tanner's large body hanging from a noose, dangling from a wrought-iron balcony overlooking the Pacific surf. By 9:45 P.M., guests had to vote for who done it on ballots provided them when they entered the castle. By 10 P.M., we'd announce the resolution of the crime and award prizes, then dance the night away on the first night of spring 1988.

That was the plan.

With three weeks remaining before the party, *Murder in the Highlands* was sold out, but the ticket orders kept pouring in. We stretched our definition of maximum capacity to 250, but after that we stopped selling tickets and started returning checks in the mail with a printed letter thanking the sender and promising to put them on our mailing list for the next *Creative States* event. Every day, we stuffed envelopes with the apologetic letter and returned checks, turning down ticket orders from some of our best friends, leading politicians, major artists, and so forth. One man actually sent a check from Boston with a request to be picked up at the Monterey airport.

On top of the 250 tickets sold were the food and wine staffs, our board, our volunteer committee, the actors, the musicians, the Weiner family, who of course lived in the mansion, the neighborhood kids, and extraneous extras, God knows how many in all. Let's say we were hoping we could hold the crowd down to three hundred.

It's a standard with California parties that your guests will arrive fashionably late. If the stated time is 7 P.M., you could expect most folks to swing by around 8. However, by 6 P.M., an hour before opening time, crowds had begun to line up at the mansion. By 6:30 there was no holding them back, and they flooded into the stately stone courtyard, where the actors were in dress rehearsal and the food preparers still laying out breads, cheeses, and meats. At 7 P.M. the busload from San Francisco arrived, and the line of guests waiting to get in stretched from the castle all the way back to the highway, along the quarter-mile-long driveway.

Nobody really knows how many people came through the Magic Mansion by the Sea that night, except that it was far in excess of three hundred and that many in attendance got in without a ticket. (It was fairly easy. The castle had several entranceways, and the absolute chaos made it possible to slip through.)

It was the party of the year, darling, or maybe of a lifetime. The most staid bankers and judges and their wives really let their hair down as they mingled with Big Sur hippies and New Age Esalen Institute types and a large cast of hysterical zanies running around trying to murder Albion

Tanner. There was Connor O'Brien, a bartender with a body in his past, slipping Mickeys into Tanner's drinks. There was an aging former child star, Mitzi Portland, convinced that her millions of fans still love her, and a crippled former high-wire artist, Janine Carpeggio, who suffered a mysterious fall. Other characters included Harriet Paul, the nosy neighbor; One Punch Polachelli, a punch-drunk former prize fighter; Inspector Harley Davidson, a police homicide detective; Wendell Wilson, an Irish tenor from Oklahoma; Evelyn Adam, a demented Christian hitchhiker; and Yabo Jocko, a washed-up comedian, who said of Albion Tanner, "He's so ugly, when he was born the doctor slapped his mother."

Bodies were crammed in shoulder to shoulder in every room of the mansion and in outdoor courtyards and grounds. The buffet was promptly gobbled up by the voracious throng, and we ran out of food by 8 P.M. Our board members took to Ellen Weiner's pantry and freezer and began serving everything in her larder to the guests, who kept coming in waves. Ten, twenty, thirty cases of wine were served by the glass until it ran out at 9:15 P.M., and a prominent plastic surgeon and member of our board, Frank Stark, made an emergency run to the nearest supermarket for another twenty cases.

Meanwhile, the cast did a terrific job of keeping the crowd involved with the story, against impossible odds. It was amazing that anyone could even hear over the high-decibel roar of the riotous throng. Then there was the matter of somehow getting Albion Tanner out of sight long enough to be murdered and tossing his ample corpse over the balcony on a rope. The first sight of the cadaver started a crowd scream that rose into the night like firecrackers on the Fourth of July, climaxing in a kind of group hysteria I'd never seen anywhere, not even in the most ardent '60s demonstrations.

There's a very fine line beyond which a party gets out of hand, ceases to be fun, maybe even attracts a visit from the police. We had the forethought to contact the state police and advise them in advance of the party and anticipated traffic jams, and they were cooperative and pleasant. We pushed fever to the bursting point and somehow, by sheer luck, managed to escape without anyone getting hurt. But we took dreadful chances.

The people jammed into the baronial living room, shrieking and screaming as the prizes were announced. Never had two tickets to Palm Springs elicited such pandemonium and joy. The last guest didn't leave until daybreak, and we spent the night in the Highlands Inn rather than try to find our car.

The reputation of *Murder in the Highlands* and press coverage that followed it was so great that the cast formed a kind of Murder, Inc., company and hired itself out to stage murders all over the state. And *Creative States* walked away with a budget for the third annual Writers' Jamboree and a commitment from Judith Martin, who writes the "Miss Manners" syndicated column, to attend.

"Miss Manners is coming, Miss Manners is coming. Quick, which fork is for dessert?" Judith Martin is actually a novelist and longtime *Washington Post* reporter, but she found her real niche with the etiquette column. After radicals like Tom Robbins and Jessica Mitford, she seemed a highly unlikely guest of the Writers' Jamboree, but she did say yes and agreed to appear for our standard fee of a percentage of the profits, if any. (In other words, nothing if none.)

Of course, it helped that Judith Martin's former college roommate, Carla Selby, is the sister of Vic Selby, who's the husband of Shayna Selby, who's a member of our board. We cut a deal based more on friendship than business.

The third annual Writers' Jamboree in November 1988 stretched the event from a day-long thing to a three-day festival, with two evening parties, four seminars on Saturday, four workshops on Sunday, two writers' lunches, and one gourmet luncheon with Miss Manners. We promoted the thing nationally at the American Booksellers Association's annual convention and in *Writers' Digest* and other publications. Our guest speakers in addition to Miss

Manners included David Stanford, editor at Viking/Penguin publishers in New York; Amanda Spake, senior editor of the *Washington Post Magazine*; Eden Ross Lipson, children's book editor of the *New York Times Book Review*; Robert Wilson, book editor of *USA Today* in Washington, D.C.; literary agents Michael Larsen and Elizabeth Pomada; Hollywood screenwriters Madeline DiMaggio and Alan Marcus; mystery novelists Robert W. Campbell and Robert Irvine; and top editors and writers from San Francisco and Los Angeles. Altogether, we accommodated thirty-two out-of-town speakers in luxury hotels and attracted the sponsorship of sixteen different wineries, a new record for writers' drinking habits in Monterey.

The opening sessions at Carmel's La Playa Hotel, a mansion built for the Ghirardelli family of San Francisco, burst into an intensely hostile exchange between the new owners of *Monterey Life* magazine and the National Writers Union local number seven. Editor George Fuller had been fired and the magazine sold to investors from L.A., who allegedly reprinted material from back issues of *Monterey Life* without securing permission from the writers. The owners denied any willful wrongdoing, and at this writing the whole affair is still in federal courts with no final judgment.

But we'd come a long way from the easy camaraderie of the first Jamboree, for better or worse. Rivalries and enemies existed where harmony and unity had been. Miss Manners was no piece of cake either, changing her plane reservations three or four times, demanding first-class tickets, changing her date of arrival, causing her hosts all manner of worrisome aggravations. Literary stars, like opera singers, are entitled to a certain amount of prima donna behavior.

Noel Young, editor of Capra Press in Santa Barbara, inspired participants with his down-to-earth comments on the business of small presses, while David Stanford of Viking/Penguin invited dozens of local writers to send him their manuscripts. (And they did, and he read every one, and to my knowledge none of them got published.) The biggest workshop crowds went for the literary agents ("pitch your book idea to literary agents") and the screenwriters. For some reason, millions of people assume they can get rich writing for TV and movies. They can't, of course, or L.A. wouldn't be full of scriptwriters waiting on restaurant tables for a living.

The least popular workshop was the wine writers' gathering hosted by *San Francisco Chronicle* wine critic Rod Smith. The cost of the workshop included hors d'oeuvres and a blind tasting of six excellent California chardonnays, but nary a soul bought a ticket. We had to give away a dozen tickets, and even some of those people didn't show up. The lesson learned, perhaps, is that while many people enjoy wine, few aspire to writing about it professionally.

Miss Manners' gourmet luncheon was an embarrassment. How could it be otherwise, we later realized, when you expose yourself to the scrutiny of the world's most proper woman? The lunch tickets at $100 each (for a lavish spread at the Highlands Inn and special wines introduced by the winemaker) were a very slow seller; only twenty-five people attended this expensive fete, and in the end we lost several thousand dollars on Miss M. A gentleman diner asked Miss Manners for advice on the proper etiquette to observe in a nudist colony—clearly a question meant to be more titillating than useful. At least nobody complained about the food.

The Writers' Jamboree Ball featured another literary play, *Spies vs. Counterspies*, with the cast of *Murder in the Highlands*. A Vice President Quaylebent was nearly assassinated, and I was physically tossed out of the Monterey Plaza Ballroom by "Secret Service guards."

The usual throngs showed up and the band played on, but something had snapped. Writers are too neurotic, too basically insecure, to have a good time together unless they get drunk. Then they boast of higher advances and sharper agents than thou, as if each of them was in direct competition with the others. "It was a dark and stormy night" as we cleaned up the postmidnight leftover wines and nursed ego-wounds. We wondered, whither Jambo?

BOOK III
BEYOND THE REVOLUTION

Chapter 11

Whatever Became of Whatshisname? Characters from *Famous Long Ago*

THE TWENTIETH ANNIVERSARY of Total Loss Farm in July 1988 called for a whale of a party, a three-day-and-night extravaganza with staged theatricals, music, picnics, camping, newspaper reporters, and a vast, sweltering reunion of all—nearly all—the lost souls who once called it home.

Some of us didn't survive, while others got lost and never found again. Marshall Bloom had been dead for nineteen long years already, hard to believe. What happened to our carpenter and New Age artist, Laurie Dodge, was in its own way even harder. Laurie was always a bit eccentric—well, *crazy* is the word. He'd been studied by psychiatrists and hospitalized in the loony bin, but no force on earth could contain his explosive energy.

He built marvelous structures from raw materials, two hands, and boundless inspiration. He converted our garage-workshop shed into a tightly insulated living room with multilevel stage for concerts, plays, and dining. He played the grand piano long into the night, knew all the classics and really loved them. With long, tangled red hair and a full beard, he appeared Christlike in his intensity. No one who met Laurie ever forgot him.

He'd take off in his truck, disappear for days or weeks, live like a native forest animal under the trees in the wild, make fires, and eat berries. Even at the farm, he sometimes slept in a snowbank and appeared winter mornings with icicles gleaming from his beard. He raved on, reciting poetry, calling everyone outside to witness the Northern Lights.

And one day he simply drove the truck to New York City, where witnesses saw him veer off the road and smash into a guardrail on the Henry Hudson Parkway near the George Washington Bridge. Appearing dazed and perhaps bloodied, he got out of the truck and ran away from the scene of the accident, climbing over a chain-link fence, on-lookers said. And he was never seen or heard from again.

The people at the farm as well as his anguished parents in Portsmouth, New Hampshire, spared no time or expense in searching for Laurie. They checked every lead, every mental hospital, morgue, police record, hippie neighbor-hood, shelter, for months and then years and *nothing*. Not a trace. No body, no person, in the end no hope. He could have been struck with amnesia after a blow to the head—why else wouldn't he get in touch?—and be alive somewhere, living another life. He was young, in good health, and capable of surviving even wilderness conditions.

Or he could be dead, an unknown corpse somewhere, never identified, long ago buried. The agony of not knowing is something we've all learned to live with, but it took its toll on our good cheer and youthfulness. We aged too fast.

But most of us aged as well as could be expected. The reunion of old friends was pleasant and hearty. The old apple tree was still there, although some of the forest has been eaten away by acid rain over Vermont—a nightmare we could scarcely have imagined back in 1968, an evil force bigger than nature and deadly as sin. The old Groll Cemetery, officially full for a century, rested primly in its grove of thick maples. The farmhouse was still on the hilltop, still in grave need of repair, but the peach orchard cresting the meadow no longer bore fruit.

The residents didn't farm at the farm, but that's only common sense. If it were possible to make a living running a family farm in Vermont, the old-timers would still be doing it. They're not. They sold out to skiers. The people on the farm kept gardens for their own enjoyment and nutrition, but they had jobs in the towns and made a living like anyone else. Nearby Brattleboro had evolved in twenty years from a one-cow backwater to a sizzling center of culture and business in a hip, sophisticated community. Brattleboro had the most popular gay bar in Vermont, Colors, owned by a former communard from the Baby Farm, Fritz Hewitt. Fritzie inherited a bit of money when his father passed away, invested in fixer-upper Brattleboro real estate, and now rents to the boys in the band.

The people at the farm were the same people who started out there twenty years earlier, and that's remarkable in itself. The place turned out to be as solid as the great oaks and ashes. Various and sundry farm people, myself included, return for sabbaticals and visits. A few new people are around too, but the board of directors of our nonprofit corporation has remained a list of familiar names.

The population at the farm was way down, however. Gone are the days of eighteen people sleeping in the one house. The tendency now is for each little nuclear family or couple to have its own house or cottage, with the whole group gathering occasionally in the grand living room. Communal dinners still happen but not with nightly regularity. Everybody's got a different schedule and responsibilities. Everybody's older now, and our children have become the dreamers of the farm. The kids get together, leave us to our elderliness, think we're old fogies.

If it sounds like a cop-out, a life without the verve and danger of our youth, then so be it. We haven't changed our ideals, but you just can't go on childlike in your innocence, trying to make a living dipping candles, sure that the New Age is around the corner. Not after Nixon, Reagan, Bush, Watergate, Irangate, Three Mile Island, Chernobyl, the greenhouse effect, and AIDS. You have to get out there, famous long ago again, and work to make your life productive and happy.

I can't precisely recall at what age this work ethic got started; it didn't happen overnight but kinda crept up on me. It happens to baby boomers when their first parent dies. You realize you have one more parent to bury, then your own number comes up. You realize you've got one foot in the grave already so you might as well have a hell of a good time with what's left. But you know that the world won't give it to you on a halcyon cloud of karmic goodness. You have to work and do your best. You have to put out. And don't forget to brush and floss after every meal. Don't smoke, drink moderately, don't eat between meals, exercise regularly, get a good night's sleep.

By July 1989, the farmhouse was completely gone, torn down and carted away. Just a year after the great twentieth-anniversary gathering, Verandah and husband Richard Coutant essentially purchased ("for the consideration of One or More Dollars") an acre of land from the Monteverdi Artists Collaborative, Inc., the nonprofit artists' organization that has owned the farm since I deeded it over in 1973. Their acre contained the farmhouse and barn and small cabins all located at the crossing of Packer's Corners Road with the Old County Road, both dirt highways.

The old farmhouse had fallen into hopeless and dangerous decrepitude, but the bank wouldn't loan money for constructing a new house to a nonprofit corporation. Verandah and Richard were thus obliged, in a way, to become private owners of the land in order to finance rebuilding a house. Earlier, Richard Wizansky, who originally came to the farm with Laurie Dodge and later married his physician, Dr. Todd, had established a precedent by purchasing with Dr. Todd a similarly small piece of land from the nonprofit foundation and had finished a fine new home with three bathrooms. Total Loss no more, the farm has gone upscale, moving away from communal ideals and artistic cooperatives and toward private ownership, mortgage payments, grown-up responsibilities.

Still, it was a bit shocking to see the ancient farmhouse destroyed, plank by beam. Richard Wizansky mailed me snapshots of the dismemberment and copies of the legal documents transferring the Monteverdi Artists' property to private ownership. In addition to the warranty deed, there was a complicated lease agreement in which the new owners leased back some of the buildings and the barn to the non-profit artists' group, with the artists paying part of the taxes and insurance costs. The terms of the lease were "perpetual, running as long as grass grows and the sun shines," the document read.

(This clause revealed a touching faith in Mother Nature. We do live in a time, however, when we can imagine the grass *not* growing and the sun *not* shining; for example, in the aftermath of nuclear war or chemical pollution so toxic that it forces us into artificial living space with canned oxygen piped in. Horrifying, yes, but believable.)

Despite the perpetual nature of the lease, the landlords can evict the artists if they don't make their tax and insurance payments within five days of the due date, can "repossess by force, summary proceedings, ejectment or otherwise," and that's the bottom line. Owners can evict, tenants can only pay.

Meanwhile, the changes at the Vermont farm were of consuming interest to artist John Wilton, who played an important role in the LNS heist and lived at the LNS farm in Montague, Massachusetts, purchased by Bloom and Steve Diamond in 1968, but has long since moved to New York City.

Johnny was one of seven people named on the deed after Marshall Bloom willed the Montague farm to what he called the Fellowship of Religious Youth, or FRY. ("You've heard of 'burn baby burn,' well, 'fry baby fry!'" Bloom liked to joke.) The place had been solely owned by Bloom and was never incorporated or given to a nonprofit organization.

The other six heirs were Steve Diamond, Cathy Hutchison, James Tapley, Harvey Wasserman, Steve Marsden, and Michael Curry, all residents at the farm in 1968, but none of them had lived there in years. They formed a Fellowship of Religious Youth Realty Trust, naming themselves as beneficiaries, with a complicated set of rules of membership. Specifically, a trustee lost his membership if he ceased living at the farm in Montague or some other place operated by FRY. The trust was supposed to dissolve itself in 1980 but was renewed. In fact, none of the trustees is religious or youthful anymore, and FRY hasn't really done anything as a religion, but it did evolve into the Muse Foundation, producers of the No Nukes concert and movie, and Green Mountain Post Films, active in the antinuclear power movement. The folks who actually live on the farm, including Janice Frey and her daughter, Sequoia, are never mentioned in the trust.

Any one of the trustees could conceivably force the sale of the farm by demanding his or her one-seventh equity in cash. The FRY board could add new members by a three-fifths vote and simply include the current farm residents. A new nonprofit corporation could replace FRY. Any of these possibilities could happen; meanwhile, the farm is owned by absentee landlords.

Looking over the past twenty years while zooming forth into the 1990s, I find the faces the same. It's only the modus operandus that's changed. Already in this hit-and-run odyssey, I've considered, reencountered, quoted, interviewed, or otherwise had relations with Marshall Bloom and his ghost, Liberace, Memere, my father, Angus Mackenzie, Alicia Bay Laurel, Bala-Bala, Jerry Rubin, Abbie Hoffman (RIP), Steve Diamond, Verandah Porche, Bob Dylan, Paul Williams, Laura Huxley, Danny Santiago, Ephraim Doner, Clint Eastwood, Robert Redford, James Leo Herlihy, Sydney Omarr, Jim Jordan, Ilili, Bob Norris, Laurie Dodge, John Wilton, Sluggo Wasserman, Peter Simon, David Sterritt, Honey Williams, Camilo Wilson, Robert Anton Wil-

son, Ken Kesey, Tom Robbins, Kurt Vonnegut, Jill Kre-
mentz, Barbara Yamaguchi, George Fuller, Jessica Mitford,
Mark Dowie, Amy Rennert, Claire Braz-Valentine, Robert
Gover, Thomas Farber, Richard Miller, Don Pendleton,
Gerald Rosen, Armistead Maupin, Robert W. Campbell, and
Judith Martin, Miss Manners.

And that's only the beginning. . . . The last years of the
1980s, with their sizable nostalgia for Woodstock, the Who,
Tommy, Rolling Stones, and Paul McCartney and everybody
celebrating the twentieth anniversary of When It All Came
Together, gave me a chance to compare notes on survival
with old friends. Those who survived, that is.

It wasn't always easy locating the original characters of
Famous Long Ago, but I spent a great deal of time and effort
trying to find and talk to every one. A couple of people just
flat-out disappeared from the face of the earth, or at any rate
hundreds of former friends didn't know where to find them.
Where, indeed, did Bala-Bala go? She was the mysterious
Barbara Heimlich who helped Bloom and me get LNS
started, and when last heard from, she was living with Eldridge Cleaver in Oakland, in 1968. If you find her, won't
you give her my love and tell her for me that it's all the same.

~

Eldridge Cleaver himself has been in the news from time to
time, but for all the wrong reasons—a shoplifting arrest, a
Christian conversion, a sales campaign for men's trousers
with an old-fashioned codpiece in the crotch, then a rape
conviction. In *Famous Long Ago* he appeared to John Wilton
and me as a kind of saint when he told us that "some people
who call themselves revolutionaries will do worse things
than any cop and do them in the name of revolution." Those
words and that attitude directly influenced our decision to
abandon the Vulgar Marxists and the Movement and set out
for utopian green fields.

If our idols, some of them anyway, proved to be only
human, how can we level blame? It's quite rare to find a
person living at the same divinely insane level of conscious-

ness that we shared twenty years ago, but Paul Krassner is one such. One and only.

~

Paul Krassner is a living legend of the counterculture. Born in 1933, he is a generation older than the baby boomers, but like Abbie Hoffman, his close friend, he led us younger radicals into the fray. In 1958 he began publishing *The Realist* magazine, which bravely took on all kinds of taboo subjects and supported outré causes such as abortion, atheism, pornography. Its circulation peaked at more than one hundred thousand copies by the late 1960s, but it went out of business in the 1970s and has just been revived as a quarterly newsletter available from P.O. Box 1230, Venice, California 90294. (Send two dollars for a sample issue.) We found Krassner at the main post office in Venice on a sunny November afternoon and repaired to his Bohemian ocean-front apartment after a quick lunch at the Sidewalk Cafe.

RM: When you did your stand-up comedy routine, was it called "Paul Krassner on Stage" or did you have some other name for it?

PK: The name I used came from Harry Reasoner's memoirs, where he says that there are only two people in his entire career he would refuse to shake hands with. One was Senator Joe McCarthy, the other was me. Which is so ironic, because I started out making fun of McCarthy—it just got me mad, because McCarthy always had senatorial immunity, and I always had to take the consequences of what I did. Reasoner said, "Krassner not only attacked Establishment values, he attacked decency in general." The name of my show was "Attacking Decency in General." I still want to get a photo of him shaking hands with me, so I can use it in my book.

RM: Would he do it?

PK: Nah. Somebody was going to arrange a party where we'd both be, but it never worked out.

RM: You were noted for attacking decency in general.

Would you say the early days of *The Realist* were essentially a kamikaze assault on what most people would consider sacred values? Walt Disney characters fornicating, Lyndon Johnson fucking the exit wound on John F. Kennedy's corpse . . .

PK: But those weren't the early days. That was in the mid-sixties, when it was at its peak, and it started in 1958. I thought that my *targets* had attacked decency, my standards of decency, so this was just self-defense.

RM: Well, here we are in the Venice apartment of Paul Krassner looking out at the blue, *blue* Pacific where a white sailboat is tilting its way across the horizon. . . .

PK: Gee, I wish I could write like that. I don't have any style. "I open the door." Another writer says, "The doorknob had a gemlike quality whose touch reminded you of first immersing . . ."

RM: But I think you're the *funniest* writer I ever met.

PK: I substitute humor for description. Humor is my religion. Everybody has to have some spiritual path, even if it's Satanism or nonbelief. And humor is the way I see the world.

RM: Do you still see some of those people from the sixties? What I'm trying to do is retrace the original characters from *Famous Long Ago*. Abbie's obviously no longer with us. Do you see Jerry Rubin?

PK: I did see Abbie. If he was alive now, we'd still be in contact. Jerry, the last time I saw him was at the Abbie memorial in New York, and we've kind of drifted apart. Well, Abbie and I were intimate friends. Jerry and I were political allies who respected each other but who didn't hang around together much.

RM: I went to one of Rubin's salons in New York. Not recently, I'd say about 1980 or '81. He was doing these networking salons where you got a beautifully printed invitation to Jerry Rubin's place. You had to wear a tie and jacket.

PK: That's why I didn't go!

RM: I didn't own a tie or jacket, so I called him and asked,

"Do I *have* to wear a tie and jacket?" and he said, "Yes, you have to," and I managed to borrow one.

PK: And you had to have a business card! I didn't have a business card. The invitation said, "Bring someone who's rich, famous, or a leader in the field," and my plan was to rent a horse, the leader in the field.

RM: Have you been in touch with Dick Gregory?

PK: Yeah, usually I'll see him at a New Age fair or something like that, and it's always a good reunion. He's in Plymouth, Massachusetts, or around there, but for all I know he could be making house calls on obese people around the world.

RM: I'm looking for Malcolm Boyd; do you remember him?

PK: Just saw him recently at a rally against the Jesse Helms amendment here in L.A., so he might be local.

RM: He had a book called *Are You Running With Me, Jesus?* in 1966-67, when he appeared on campus at Boston University. Malcolm and I went to Vietnam together—no, we met the North Vietnamese and the Vietcong at a conference in Czechoslovakia. He also came out as a gay Episcopal priest.

PK: His next book is going to be *Are You Swishing with Me, Jesus?*

RM: Do you remember Shirley Clarke, the filmmaker?

PK: Sure, but I don't know where she went. She may still be at the Chelsea Hotel. If she's alive; I'm not sure. You know how sometimes you have that funny feeling that somebody died, but you're not sure?

RM: Stokely Carmichael?

PK: He married Miriam Makeba, that's all I know. They could even be divorced by now. "I couldn't stand that clicking, man."

RM: Mel Lyman?

PK: He was a junior Manson. [Pause, sound of inhaling. "Excellent quality, man." "Hmmm." "Righteous stuff."] Let's take turns. Tell me about the trip in Washington, that college editors' conference, wasn't it?

RM: Yes. I remember the time you were in Washington. You were and Jerry and Abbie and others from the counterculture were invited as guests of the United States Student Press Association. Marshall Bloom and I had been directors of that group but we were ousted, or should I say Bloom was ousted and I resigned in protest. David Lloyd Jones became the international director of USSPA and he was our buddy, so it was Bloom who convinced him to invite all these crazy freaks to the conference at some major hotel in Washington. Eugene McCarthy was running for president and was scheduled to speak.

PK: Right, I was supposed to introduce him. And then his advisers told him that wouldn't be a good idea.

RM: That's an interesting wrinkle on the story. Anyway, we were afraid of Eugene McCarthy basically because we were afraid he was going to take our people away from us. He was just antiwar enough to have a lot of appeal to naive young people, whereas Bloom and I considered ourselves professional radicals.

PK: When you say "our people" what do you mean?

RM: Young, stoned people.

PK: The Yippies at this point had already been formed?

RM: Yes, and Jerry considered himself the unofficial leader of the Yippies and went there representing the Yippies. Bloom and I of course represented Liberation News Service. We were not taken with Eugene McCarthy. He wasn't radical enough for us. He was not even against the war, not for "unilateral withdrawal from Vietnam."

PK: Exactly.

RM: So he was more liberal than Lyndon Johnson and was regarded as sort of a great white hope by the college kids. We decided we had to do everything possible to destroy this guy's image in the eyes of the college editors. David Lloyd Jones arranged for the room to go black at one point, and this crazy film came on with all these images of napalmed babies and bombs dropping superimposed on the wall, and everybody freaked out. Then an actor, posing as a college editor, stood up and started screaming that he'd been in Vietnam and the rest of us didn't know shit, just white-assed college kids who didn't know the reality of Vietnam.

PK: He fooled me, though. I stood on a chair. "You wouldn't call him a commie," I yelled out.

RM: Jerry started yelling, "The Yippies did it, the Yippies did it!" Which of course wasn't true; David Lloyd Jones did it, this planned disruption, but Jerry got credit for it. All the newspapers the next day said the Yippies did it.

PK: This scene is also in my book, my unauthorized autobiography called *The Winner of the Slow Bicycle Race.*

RM: David Lloyd Jones really got in a lot of trouble because the U.S. Student Press Association did not find this amusing. He had spent ten thousand dollars in a grant from the *Washington Post.* Lloyd Jones lost his job, but it was great guerrilla theater.

PK: It really was. If it could fool us . . .

RM: And Eugene McCarthy was absolutely vanquished. He was giving a speech from the podium when a whole bunch of freaks started walking down the aisle carrying a coffin . . .

PK: Covered with "McCarthy for President" buttons!

RM: Right, and stuffed with those buttons.

PK: But Jerry, who was still on acid, had this newspaper with a headline saying "2,000 Vietnamese Freed by Cong," and he didn't know whether he should interrupt McCarthy. I told him, "Just do it," without realizing I was inspiring his book title *Do It!* So he went up on stage and asked McCarthy if he thought it was a good thing.

RM: And McCarthy just *ran* out of that room.

PK: Yeah. In my book I describe how on the way to that conference, we got off the train in Washington, and Bobby Kennedy, who was still not running, got off the train and was just standing there talking to an aide. Abbie, Jerry, and I were like the Three Stooges, going "What are we gonna do?" I had once sent a magazine article on American atrocities in Vietnam to every person in the Senate and Bobby Kennedy was the only one I got a response from, so I figured he was at least better than the rest. At least he acknowledged that he got it. So I stood there thinking, "Why should I do something?" but Jerry with his left brain was saying, "We got to do something. He's standing right there. Look at how tan and handsome he is!" And Abbie, who is all right brain, went ten or fifteen yards away from him and yelled at him, "Bobby, you got no guts!"

RM: Did he react?

PK: As I put it in my book, "The senator flinched ever so slightly."

RM: Are you reissuing *The Realist*?

PK: Yes, in newsletter form. I'll give you some copies. [He produces a copy of *The Realist* with a cartoon cover depicting Mighty Mouse snorting coke, Bugs Bunny smoking a joint, Gumby shooting heroin, Superman sucking on a water pipe, etc., in the "Hop Den."]

RM: Didn't you once have over one hundred thousand subscribers?

PK: It was over one hundred thousand all together, subscribers, bookstores, and newsstands combined, but it may have reached over a million people with pass-on readership and library subscriptions.

RM: Libraries subscribed to *The Realist*? That's great, but I find it hard to believe.

PK: Oh, yeah. Librarians liked it, and they kept getting replacement copies because they kept getting stolen.

RM: When did it go out of business, and when did it come back?

PK: It was published from '58 to '74, when I got the Feminist Party Media Workshop award for humor, wit, courage, and longevity in journalism, and that was the month it stopped publishing. And then it started again as a newsletter in '85 after a little eleven-year hiatus.

RM: Nothing at all. So, how is the new book coming along? Is it going to bring us up to date on all your misadventures?

PK: It covers fifty years, from 1939 to 1989.

RM: Was '39 the year of your birth?

PK: No, it was the year I woke up, at the age of six. That's the first sentence of the book: "I first woke up at the age of six." It's a real educational process. I'll tell you something, Ray. Well, you know, you've done autobiography; at the same time you have total indulgence in your ego, it's also total separation from your ego.

RM: I know.

PK: So to find your balance between those is a real trip.

RM: Trying to tell the truth is hard.

PK: I know because you peel off a layer and say, oh wait, there's another layer underneath that. I find myself revealing stuff to strangers that I haven't shared with intimate friends. And I still remember my father's voice, when he used to count the number of times the word *I* was used in an article. I keep saying to him, to the grave, "Dad, I'm writing in the first person, what else can I do?" What else can *one* do? Emmett Grogan wrote the first half of his book in the third person.

RM: And the second half in the first person?

PK: Yes, the person was Kenny Wisdom, then he switched it to Emmett Grogan.

RM: Was that his novel *Ringolevio*?

PK: Yes, that's being republished by Dan Levy at Citadel Press. He wanted to republish my book too, a collection from *The Realist*, but a lot of that stuff is old, the writing is embarrassing, and some of it is material I use in the autobiography, so I don't want it to seem like I'm rehashing.

RM: Levy has gotten into a little bit of trouble with some people complaining that all the books in the *Citadel Underground Classics* series are by guys, no chicks. [Since this interview, a number of women were added.]

PK: Well, the women's movement just began to develop in 1969. I went to the first Miss America Day parade. I would have still been friends with Robin Morgan, but that was my first political expulsion. We were close friends, and then she said I would no longer be welcome in her house if I continued writing for *Cavalier* magazine. I was their film critic, but it was a girlie magazine. Meanwhile, she was working for Grove Press. I was supporting my daughter, and it was an insane request. That happened in 1970, when feminism was just breaking through. [The phone rings, and Krassner lets his answering machine answer it.]

RM: Do you want to pick that up?

PK: No, that's what the machine is for. Bless 'em. I actually cut the wires to my phone once, when I was living in Watsonville [California].

RM: Tell me about Watsonville. I heard somebody say you were living there, and I thought that an unlikely place.

PK: That's when I had just moved from New York, '71 to '75. Ken Kesey and I had edited that last supplement to the *Whole Earth Catalog*, and I met these Merry Pranksters who found this place on a cliff overlooking the ocean. I had never even heard of Watsonville. There was a deserted beach, and I just fell in love with the place. It was paradise for a city boy. It was one of my happiest times and scariest times, since that's when I started getting involved with studying conspiracies and the Charles Manson case. Pretty spooky. And my good friend Lee Quanstrom, who was an old Prankster, was working for the *Watsonville Register-Pajaronian*. He brought acid consciousness to this small-town paper.

RM: I worked for the *Carmel Pine Cone*, and they totally embraced me. They let me write anything I wanted. I had a wonderful time writing my own weekly column, being invited out to eat in restaurants and stay in posh hotels for free.

PK: That's the kind of thing you'd do for free if you were independently wealthy.

RM: Absolutely. I met a very wealthy lady from Oyster Bay, New York, who offered to write a column for the *Pine Cone* free of charge because she wanted the social entrée. I got tired of doing it though the pay wasn't that bad, not enough to live on but a nice supplement, but I just got really tired of churning the thing out.

PK: I had an ideal job working for *Cavalier* doing movie reviews once a month. I got to pick the movies. I started one off, "I have now seen *Midnight Cowboy* twice. The first time, I took mescaline. The second time, I took notes." I had that kind of freedom. But after a while it bothered me because I didn't want to predispose the readers to my insights. So I'd start off, "Go see this movie with a friend, and *then* come back and read this." A good book or movie should unfold, so when you know what's coming it's no good.

RM: Well, in reviewing books, especially novels, I always make it a point not to reveal the whole plot. I'll even say something like, "Whether or not this entanglement will succeed for James depends on his mother's will," or something like that. What about show biz? Have you been writing scripts here in Los Angeles?

PK: No, not primarily. I was the head writer for an HBO special in 1980, making fun of the election campaign. What was so frustrating was that the script got so watered down that it drove me back to doing stand-up comedy. The actors, producers, director, everybody wanted to get in on watering down the script. This was HBO's first venture into outside production. On stage it's just you, the microphone, and the audience, and you don't have all these other filters in between.

RM: We need you to do that since we don't have Lenny Bruce anymore.

PK: I do feel I'm carrying on the tradition.

RM: And I can't think of anyone else who does. There are a lot of comics around . . .

PK: But they all do jokes about shopping in the 7-Eleven or old TV shows, and they all want to get on Johnny Carson or Letterman or Arsenio Hall, and get their own sit-com. One kid said to me he was going into stand-up because he heard comedy is a well-paying profession. So I said, "But don't you *have* to be funny?" But he thought of it as a career move. They wind up imitating each other's style.

RM: Do you think young people are really different from the way we were?

PK: They all have an MTV attention span. I don't want to generalize, but a lot of them do.

RM: They don't have the draft to worry about. The draft was a big motivation to us in the sixties. Our bodies were on the line. Fuck up once and you could be right over there in Vietnam getting shot at.

PK: Absolutely true. Now the *contras* are toy soldiers. Wind them up and they fight. Ours was also an affluent time, and you could really live cheaply.

RM: The assumption was that the nation would just get more and more prosperous. You read this a lot nowadays. You read baby boomers are depressed because they grew up in the sixties in a time of seemingly endless prosperity, then in the seventies they had to realize that things were getting steadily worse, and by the eighties they knew they couldn't afford their own home or the things their parents had, that the U.S. standard of living was actually going backwards.

PK: New York is like a Third World country now. I don't know if you remember Jerome Washington, Jay Washington. He was one of the first black Yippies, and he was married to Ellen Maslow. He just got out of prison after seventeen years on a frame murder charge, and I spoke to him on Bob Fasset's show on WBAI, on the air. I asked him what his biggest culture shock was, and he said, "The look of desperation on the faces of people in New York City, even the young people." And coming from someone who'd been behind bars for seventeen years, it was startling.

RM: What about abortion? I thought we had the abortion issue completely won after Roe v. Wade, but now it's come back. Do you ever hear from [abortion activist] Bill Baird?

PK: No, I've only seen him on television.

RM: That's a point where our lives crossed. When I was first in touch with Baird, it was through you. You had published something about his abortion clinic in Long Island in *The Realist*, and I called you to reach Baird. I reached him and brought him to the Boston University campus, where he passed out condoms and vaginal foams in front of a huge rally of two thousand students and got arrested for violating the "crimes against chastity."

PK: That should be a title of a book. What was the outcome?

RM: The outcome was that Baird overthrew the Massachusetts birth control laws. It took years and lengthy trials, but he won in the end.

PK: I was paying his rent at his clinic. He might have been something of a nut, but everybody I helped was a nut. Madalyn Murray, the atheist. You don't get American Gothic-type straight people to do these crusades.

RM: Well, Baird took on women's reproductive rights as an absolute personal mission, and he's still doing it.

PK: His identity was completely tied up with it. He convinced himself it was his calling.

RM: Do you remember when you wrote an essay for the *BU News* about impeaching Lyndon Johnson? I was the editor and put together a panel of what I considered experts to write about the subject, all of whom agreed with my point of view that he should be impeached. Your piece was called "Impeach His Own." It was page-one news in the *New York Times* the next day, "Boston University student newspaper calls for impeachment of the president." This was 1967, and it was considered outrageous. Nobody had called for impeaching the president since Andrew Johnson. The president of Boston University sent individual telegrams to every member of Congress, deploring the editorial and pointing out that most students at BU didn't agree with the tiny faction of radicals editing the paper. The funny thing was that we had announced we were going to mail the editorial to every member of Congress, but we didn't have to do it, since his telegram took care of informing them about it. We saved the postage.

PK: That story is in my book too. I don't want to duplicate the same story from your book.

RM: That's OK, just write it in your own inimitable style. I never met a story I couldn't embellish a little anyway. Not the big lie, of course.

PK: The way I work a story is I go on stage with only seven or eight words on a page, areas I'm going to get into. It's a mixture of telling stories I've told before and starting new ones. Something that was a one-liner one week may be three minutes long a week later. And as a story that starts out true gets embellished and embellished, I could pass a lie-detector test. After I've told a story so many times, it's a construct of truth in my mind. I could pass a lie-detector test saying that I snorted cocaine with the pope. I've envisioned it, I've described it. That's why I don't think they should allow hypnotic testimony in the courtroom from witnesses who have been hypnotized.

RM: Because what they say while hypnotized is not necessarily the truth?

PK: Right, but they believe it to be the truth. So when somebody says to me, "That's not really true about your snorting cocaine with the pope, is it?" there's a split second when I'm not sure. I just made it up. Daniel Goldman wrote about this principle in *Psychology Today* that if you want to deceive other people you have to first deceive yourself. I'm sure that's what happened with Jim Bakker. He rationalized his evil. That's the purpose of fiction, because everybody can't write in the first person.

RM: Any plans of what to do after your book is finished?

PK: I want to write novels. I think this book will give me the clout to be able to do that. And screenplays. My contract says the screen rights cannot be sold except by me; I have one hundred percent of the rights. And I won't sell unless I can write the screenplay. It's bad enough if somebody fucks up your novel, but if they fuck up your life [story] . . .

RM: I had the same problem when Robert Redford bought the rights to *Famous Long Ago*. I didn't want to see it turned into one of those bad movies about the counter-culture, like *Wild in the Streets*.

PK: In that movie they put acid in the water supply. In Chicago in 1968, the mayor's assistant told us, "We've seen *Wild in the Streets*, we've seen *The Battle of Algiers*."

RM: They believed that you were capable of anything?

PK: Of dropping a bomb on an ice cream parlor where kids would be blown up. That's what their mythology was, so it was our mythology versus their mythology. I was told I was one of twenty people they finally reduced down to eight, the Chicago Eight. When I wasn't indicted, I felt like a disc jockey who wasn't offered payola.

RM: What message would you give to the youth of America today? Are kids today interested in what we went through?

PK: I've spoken to about five classes at universities, on the topic of the sixties. There's a new wave of interest. The timing is right.

~

Dick Gregory is a saint who remained pure of heart despite everything. Like Krassner, he has been a stand-up comic, but he long ago left show business to become a one-man crusade. Our LNS headquarters at 3 Thomas Circle in Washington also served as the national office of Gregory for President. And I'd vote for him today.

Toward the end of the '60s, Dick took up fasting as a way of calling attention to the problems of war and poverty, and we used to worry ourselves sick that he was going to collapse or otherwise hurt himself. Nonetheless, he shoveled

snow from our office steps on his thirtieth day of not eating.
And he is now the principal spokesman for compassion and
help for the extremely overweight. He literally, as Krassner
said, crisscrosses the nation making house calls on people
who are too fat to leave home.

"When I wrote that book called *Nigger*," he told me,
referring to his autobiography, "I figured that every time
somebody used that word, they would be giving me a free
plug!"

When I caught up with him—no easy task as this ema-
ciated guy really moves fast—Dick was in the Cedar Grove
district of Shreveport, Louisiana, in late 1989, conducting
a one-man war on drugs. The area is poverty-stricken and
had been a festering den of crack dealers until Gregory
literally set up camp in the city's A. B. Palmer Park. There's
no way to tell if his good work will permanently oust the
dealers, but already he's had a salutary effect, organizing
volunteers to clean up the area.

He likes to say, "The drug crisis is so huge, so complicated, that it makes the civil rights movement look like
child's play."

~

Tom Hayden's book *Reunion, A Memoir* may have been
unfortunately overshadowed by the scandal-sheet publicity
following his 1989 separation from actress wife Jane Fonda,
but it's a very thorough and meticulous record of all that
went down in his tumultuous career, including many verba-
tim documents from his FBI files. Tom and I first connected
when he was with the Newark Project, living in the ghetto,
and I was editing the *Boston University News*, to which he
contributed an article. He also wrote the first draft of what
became the Port Huron Statement, the founding document
of Students for a Democratic Society.

The difference between LNS and SDS was the difference between anarchism and ideological socialism, perhaps.
Hayden was also a member of an earlier generation than
ours. Born in 1939, he's pre–baby boomer. He was always

very serious and never, to my knowledge, fooled around with drugs. He's certainly earned respect from four terms as a California assemblyman representing Santa Monica, despite virulent efforts by the Republicans to have him thrown out because of his record of support for the North Vietnamese during the war. Tom and I journeyed together to meet the Vietcong in Bratislava, Czechoslovakia, in 1967. Today he's fighting for greater protection for the environment.

How does he see our generation's accomplishments?

"We accomplished more than we expected, more than most generations ever accomplish. . . . The New Left fostered a vision that gradually took hold throughout much of society. At the center of that vision was a moral view of human beings, 'ordinary people' in the process of history, a view which held that systems should be designed for human beings and not the other way around.

"I miss the sixties and always will."

～

Bill "Spaceman" Lee, former star lefthanded pitcher for the Boston Red Sox, reemerged in 1988 as a presidential candidate on the Rhinoceros Party ticket. "No guns, no butter," Lee's campaign slogan declared; "there's too much cholesterol in butter," Spaceman told an adoring audience in Cambridge, Massachusetts. He was famous for being suspended by commissioner Bowie Kuhn after admitting in public that he sprinkled marijuana on his breakfast cereal.

"I never said I 'smoked pot,' " Lee insisted. Pressed for his position on mandatory drug testing, he replied, 'I've tested mescaline. I've tested them all. But I don't think it should be mandatory!"

～

Cathy Hutchison (now Rogers) returned to her native Washington state in the early 1970s and has been a respected Seattle naturopathic doctor ever since. Cathy was the main reason I moved to Seattle myself, as she helped cure my pregnant ex-wife's hip. Ever cheerful and hardworking, she continued to house former LNS farmers at her Seattle lakeside home and recently collaborated with Verandah and Montague-based artist Susan Maraneck on an elegant handmade book.

~

James Tapley, once called Wonderboy in tandem with Mad John Wilton, fell in love with Cathy Hutchison, won her heart away from Steve Diamond, and moved with her to Seattle, where they had their son, Noah. Jamie became a first-class bookbinder, eventually; after he and Cathy broke up in 1974, he moved to San Francisco and Texas but wound up settling in Florida, where he had grown up.

~

Sam Lovejoy earned a reputation as something of a maestro extraordinaire among radical activists. He single-handedly cut down a huge nuclear power plant weather tower in Massachusetts, then won acquittal at a sensational trial in which he argued that he had acted in defense of the lives of nearby residents. Sam's exploits were detailed in the movie *Lovejoy's Nuclear War*, produced by Green Mountain Post and shown on public TV, in art film houses, and on college campuses. He organized the Musicians United for Safe Energy (MUSE) Foundation, which produced the No Nukes concert, film, and recordings from Madison Square Garden. He lived on the Liberation News Service farm in Montague for some years and now travels back and forth between New York City and Massachusetts. I reached him at his Manhattan apartment.

RM: Are you living in New York these days, Sam?
SL: I sure am. I passed the Massachusetts bar, and I'll be admitted to the New York bar soon.
RM: You're a lawyer?
SL: Oh yeah, and I've been working with Richard Coutant

on a project in Vermont; it's a lot of fun, although it might not come through. We're working on a giant water-distribution business from a natural spring in central Vermont.

RM: You mean like bottled water for the home?

SL: Yeah, everybody has to have it these days.

RM: I have it in my house, even though I now live in the Palm Springs area with plenty of good water.

SL: It's hot.

RM: I'm wondering what's happened to you since the days of *Famous Long Ago*. Some of us, like myself, remained crazy, but some people became Republicans or born-again Christians.

SL: Well, I was a founding member and organizer of the Seabrook demonstrations, the Clamshell Alliance, in '75-6-7-8 [demonstrations against the Seabrook, New Hampshire, nuclear power plant]. I traveled all over the country setting up antinuclear direct action groups.

RM: But were you part of the recent [1989] demonstrations at Seabrook?

SL: No, not recently. Then I've been doing the MUSE dance.

RM: MUSE had a dance?

SL: No, I mean doing the MUSE thing. MUSE is still in business, and I have to do little things, helping out the artists, selling syndication rights. The No Nukes movie is still in circulation out there. Let's see, then in 1982 I went back to living on the farm, in late '84 Janice and I broke up and I decided to go to law school. I traveled around Mexico for a couple of months, thinking it over, just my normal mental shakedown, retrofitting. I came back and went to law school at Western New England School of Law, became a member of the Massachusetts bar in 1988, and I've already passed the exam in New York.

RM: Very good, Sam. You sound like you've become respectable.

SL (laughing): Well, I can't tell you anything illegal because you're not printing that, right?

RM: Well, I guess we shouldn't. You're a man of property and position now. Are you specializing in any kind of legal work?

SL: Poor people, local people, a lot of pro bono work, municipal stuff. One of the things I've done a lot of, and you may get a kick out of this, several of my quote clients are in a sense former hippies—people who set up legal arrangements that are sort of quasicommunal fifteen to twenty years ago, and meanwhile the world has changed. They want to rewrite, break arrangements, change.

RM: That reminds me, isn't the Montague LNS Farm in something like that? Twenty-year-old arrangement, very idealistic, none of the trustees actually lives at the farm anymore . . .

SL: Exactly, exactly. I don't know how it's going to work out. I don't think it should become a nonprofit corporation, though. I think it should stay as a trust.

RM: The nonprofit corporation worked out for many years in Vermont, but when it turned out Verandah and Richard needed to rebuild the house, they had to own the land privately to get a bank loan. While the nonprofit thing worked for a time, it wasn't working when the farmhouse was falling down.

SL: Exactly. Everybody could have chipped in without a mortgage or bank loan, but you know, they would have built a shack, not a real house.

RM: Are we too old to live in shacks now?

SL: Absolutely!

~

Joan Baez last year brought out her autobiography, *And a Voice to Sing With*, which I reviewed for her hometown paper, the *San Francisco Chronicle*. We've seen each other many times over the years by virtue of renting houses from the same kindhearted Carmel landlady, Cynthia Williams, who was providing shelter to Joanie from the days long before she got famous. Joan's sister, singer Mimi Farina, was married to the late Richard Farina and was in Cynthia's living room the night he crashed his motorcycle.

In the book, Joan candidly reveals a long-ago lesbian affair with a young woman she rescued from the streets. They put up together at the Carmel River Inn, everybody's favorite cheap motel by the roadside on the way to Big Sur. And she admitted, with startling honesty, that her records don't sell as well today as they once did.

The memoir makes her even more attractive, not just a crusader for peace and freedom (although she continues to support myriad causes) but a real person with deep principles, a vulnerable person who grew afraid that she was ugly, who's tried to raise her son by former activist David Harris to inherit a better world.

~

Bill Kairys, a friend since college years and *Famous Long Ago*, dropped the counterculture and joined the Sufi order of mystics, changing his name to Shams. He moved to the West Coast and went to work full time for relief efforts to ease famine and cure blindness in Third World countries. Bill's mother from Pennsylvania, worried over these changes in her heretofore "normal" son, came out to California to see him. "Don't worry," I assured her, "we loved him when he was Bill and we love him as Shams, and maybe he'll be Bill again someday." To show you how the 1980s changed us (again), Shams now uses his family name as well as his Sufi one and went into the business of providing filtration systems for healthier home drinking water.

~

Honey Williams, one of the original SDS people with Tom Hayden, in much the same spirit got a real estate license so she could help her friends achieve home comfort. Since she was already deeply involved with houses, occupied with rebuilding the historic Garapata Trout Farm near Big Sur and committed to preserving high ecological standards on the central coast, it was only natural for her to go into the commerce of land and buildings. Twenty years ago, we would have gagged at the very idea of being a real estate agent, but today it's good to know a principled one.

~

Warren Hinckle, who with his eye patch and caged monkey struck a swashbuckling posture as editor of *Ramparts* magazine when Bloom and I reported the hot inside story of the Columbia University student uprising in 1968, is still in San Francisco (nominally) and still pounding the keyboard as a columnist for the *Examiner*, published by William Randolph Hearst III, who prefers to be called simply Will. The paper also publishes Hunter S. Thompson, Jan Morris, Armistead Maupin, writers too good for the newspaper trade. But if you try to contact Hinckle at his *Examiner* office, he's usually in Ireland, fomenting some kind of rebellion. He comes as close to anyone to carrying on the tradition of the late Charles McCabe, himself.

~

David Sterritt, easily the wildest of our college crowd (he was notorious for skipping classes, getting drunk, staying out all night, flunking out, etc.), married his Boston University sweetheart, Ginny, and went on to become the chief film critic of the *Christian Science Monitor*, a publication not noted for its wildness.

He lives in New York, a comfortable distance from the *Monitor* offices in Boston, with wife and twin teenage sons, Craig and Jeremy, who are precocious artists in their own right. Dinner at the Sterritts was sophisticated, delicious, good cheer. Seeing Dave Sterritt as paterfamilias left me feeling now I've seen everything, but people don't really change. Humor and mischief still come naturally to him.

~

Onetime Queen of the Bay State Poets for Peace, **Verandah Porche** was also poetry editor of Liberation News Service and is the author of *The Body's Symmetry* and other books of poems. Verandah was married for a time and had a daughter, Oona, now a tall teenager. Verandah teaches poetry to elementary school students in Vermont in the Poet in the Schools program and has lived for the past twenty-three years at the farm once called Total Loss. We interviewed her at home on the farm with her second husband, Richard Coutant, a hip lawyer and major Red Sox fan, and their six-year-old daughter, Emily. Except for the funky communal-farm backdrop, Verandah appears a perfectly normal, middle-class mother and teacher.

RM: Do you love the house now that it's almost finished? [Verandah and Richard had just completed building a new home on the site of the original farmhouse.]

RC: Yes, it's wonderful!

RM: Sam Lovejoy tells me how you and he are working together on a project to bottle and sell Vermont spring water.

RC: Well, it's sort of on the back burner. Those people are getting a divorce right now, and the business isn't their top priority!

RM: Verandah, how have you been? Congratulations on your new house.

VP: Oh, just wait and see what it's going to be like when it's finished. There will be places to evacuate, and places to lie down, and everything! [By places to evacuate she means indoor toilets instead of the old outhouse.]

RM: Last time I talked with you, I started writing the book about our crowd and what went down since LNS days. So I wonder what's new with you.

VP: Well, just this past week I did a poetry reading at a college in Woodstock, Vermont, and I ran across a former editor from Beacon Press, he was a friend of Arnold Tovell, and I swear, the guy was carrying a copy of *Famous Long Ago*. And he remembered the time when we all came down to Boston and visited the office with one of our dogs. Maybe it was Barf Barf.

RM: No, I think it was Mamoushka.

VP: That's right. Anyway, there we were talking about you and reliving that day. Marty Jezer was with us.

RM: Oh, I need to talk to Marty too.

VP: He's in Montreal, and he's writing a book about Abbie Hoffman for Rutgers University Press.

RM: Really? Aren't there several other people also working on books about Abbie?

VP: Yes, Jonah Raskin is doing one and got a large advance, two hundred thousand dollars, to write a real tell-all, gossipy book. But Marty's doing a more serious and modest book analyzing what Abbie did for the movement.

RM: Marty's a very good writer, and he'll do a solid job. I read in *Newsweek* that Jerry Rubin was offered four hundred thousand dollars for an Abbie Hoffman book, but the publishers later took it back.

VP: That's because nobody would talk to Jerry Rubin.

RM: Who would? Would you?

VP: Are you kidding? The only words he ever spoke to me were in a hotel in Washington when we were at a demonstration, and he asked if I knew where he and Paul Krassner could get laid. I said, "Certainly not."

RM: *Famous Long Ago* is being republished next year in the *Citadel Underground Classics* series. Did you ever send them the farm anthology?

VP: Yes, we got a letter from Dan Levy saying he didn't want *Home Comfort*. He wrote that he certainly enjoyed reading it, but he didn't want it for the series, blah blah blah, and asked me if I knew how to get a copy of Steve Diamond's book *What the Trees Said*.

RM: He since got a copy, but he hasn't signed that book either. He might buy it but has to wait till next year to sign more books. He did get Terry Southern, Don McNeil, and Emmett Grogan, if you remember him.

VP: Of course, I remember *Ringolevio*. Speaking of books, Mimi Morton wrote the most hilarious book we've read in years called *The Diary of Barbara Bush*, a fiction.

RM: How could she get it published?

VP: Well, it's obviously humor so there's no legal problem. But humor *is* very hard to sell these days.

RM: Do you have anything coming out soon?

VP: Yes, a big piece is coming out in the *Village Voice*, and I've started publishing poetry again. Cathy Rogers and I did that hand-made book, *Glancing Off* [a limited edition at five hundred dollars a copy].

RM: Do you know where to find Barbara Heimlich these days? And where is Gary Rader? Lisbeth Meisner?

VP: Oh, my God, these are names I haven't heard in twenty years. I haven't got the faintest idea. But what I remember is how gay the LNS and farm were, but nobody knew it. They were all in the closet. It was just horrible in those days. They could take the credibility out of anybody's ideas just by calling him a faggot. Marshall didn't live long enough to enjoy gay liberation. Everybody else came out.

~

Stephen Davis, who worked with us on the *BU News* and LNS, distinguished himself as a music writer and author of celebrity biographies. He grew up in New York during the 1950s while his father was the executive producer of the "Howdy Doody" show on network TV, so Steve had access to all the inside dirt about the show, which he published in 1988 in a book called *Say Kids, What Time Is It?* You'll be shocked to learn that the reason Clarabelle the Clown never spoke a word was that the producers didn't want to pay him a union wage for a speaking role, that Buffalo Bob and Clarabelle were mortal enemies, that Princess Summer-Fall-Winter-Spring was a foul-mouthed chorine with a disreputable past, that Clarabelle hated children and maliciously squirted the kids in the peanut gallery, and that backstage hands made the puppets do lewd and obscene gestures on (live) camera.

(Ain't it always the case? The people who work in children's programming and publishing are frequently childless and don't like children. Restaurant owners never eat the food in their own places. When I owned a bookstore, I stopped reading books. And Miss Manners never sent *Creative States* a thank you note! It's the nature of things to be contrary.)

~

Dr. Spock (Benjamin, of course, author of *Baby and Child Care* and surrogate parent to an entire generation of American kids) bailed me out of jail after the Pentagon demonstration of October 1967. As editor of LNS, I was in the front lines of the battle and wound up sharing a Lorton, Virginia, prison cell overnight with Norman Mailer, Robert Lowell, Dave Dellinger, and other leading radicals. It was not your usual bunch of jailbirds, to say the least. I still don't know how he did it, but Mailer managed to smuggle a bottle of whiskey into the cell on his person, and we all took hits through the long night. He was gregarious and loud and kept making crude jokes about women. Robert Lowell sat in the corner, quietly personifying the retiring poet. "Uncle Dave" D. was our wise pacifist leader as ever.

I was dead broke and wondering how I'd ever get out of there when the desk warden informed me my fifty-dollar bond had been paid by Dr. Benjamin Spock. He actually paid bail for dozens of other young people that day as well. And I never did repay him or even get a chance to say thanks, until now.

Today, he's eighty-six and quite well, thank you, living with his current wife, Mary Morgan, on sailboats from Camden, Maine, to the South Sea Islands. They just coauthored a new book, *Spock on Spock: A Memoir of Growing Up with the Century*, and it reveals an unknown side of this kindly giant. For example, his mother was quite a tyrant and told him, "Benny, you are not attractive looking. You just have a pleasant smile." He admits to having chosen pediatrics to please his mother and to having married strong-willed women, as well.

Of course, he was a leader in the antiwar movement and also ran for president on the People's Party ticket, although he claims he didn't really want to be the candidate but got drafted because the only two well-known people in the party were Gore Vidal and himself.

Most amazing, Dr. Spock still spends at least one day in jail per year, protesting and standing up for his beliefs. Despite a stroke and pacemaker implant two years ago, he says that he'll still "climb any barbed wire fence" to support a cause.

~

Andy Kopkind is one of the most widely published and best-known journalists and editors of the American left. In *Famous Long Ago*, he was one of the people who visited the Vietcong and North Vietnamese in the Czechoslovakia summit. Associated then with *New Times* and *The New Republic*, he is today editor of *The Nation* magazine and divides his time between New York City and a farm in Vermont located next door to Total Loss Farm.

RM: Andrew, we are pleased and surprised to find you still living in Vermont at what was called Tree Frog Farm. Presumably it's now your personal residence?

AK: Yes, well it hasn't been a communal farm for a long time. It's our official residence. John and I have sublet an apartment in the West Village in New York and spend a lot of time there; we've been in that same place for ten years, but we consider this place our real home. We bought the farm in 1974 and have been here fifteen years. There was some minor financial participation by Kathryn Kilgore, but we bought her out.

RM: Well, it's good to hear that you and John are still together.

AK: Yes, John and I have been together eighteen years now.

RM: That's great, and are you still writing?

AK: I'm still writing. I've been editor of *The Nation* since 1983, and I'm putting together a book of my coverage of the 1988 presidential campaign. Actually the book is due this morning. And technically I'm on leave from

The Nation for six months and will go back there when
the book is finished. Where are you these days?

RM: In southern California, in the high desert mountains
north of Palm Springs.

AK: Years ago, we went to Joshua Tree National Monument
and found it just wonderful with spring blooming everywhere. Then we drove back down into Palm Springs,
and it was spring break with bumper-to-bumper traffic
and college kids all over the streets. It was just horrible,
and we got out of town.

RM: Tell us what you see for the future of progressive
politics in America. Is there any hope at all? Do you
think Jesse Jackson has a chance for the presidency?

AK: No. Not really. If the Democrats get back in power, it
would be with someone like Chuck Robb, who is no
better than anyone else.

RM: How do you mean, no better?

AK: He'd do the same kinds of things the Republicans do.
I don't see any progressive movement achieving anything. It's depressing, but you just have to look at the
transformation going on around the world. The U.S.
has become the force of authoritarianism, replacing the
U.S.S.R. We'll be forced into it by Eastern Europe in
1992.

RM: In 1992, because of the economic unification of the
European Common Market?

AK: Of course. Everybody in Europe is going crazy about
1992, and Eastern Europe is a part of that. At some
point, Yalta II will reconfigure a huge geopolitical
entity, and I can't believe that America will get a piece
of it. European economic unity will be bad news for the
U.S. standard of living. There will be a lot of resent-
ment and alienation in this country, a lot of protest and
violence, which will be followed by repression. The
people who will suffer the most are the ones who always
suffer—the poor, the blacks, the ones who need social
controls.

RM: Sounds pretty grim.

AK: Just look at how the U.S. standard of living has re-
gressed and declined in the last twenty years. The income of the average American household is about what
a single male could earn twenty years ago.

RM: That's a startling statistic.

AK: Remember, that's the average. The middle class is still
scrambling to acquire all kinds of consumer things,
which requires keeping meaningless rote jobs. The
schools get more horrible all the time. Big companies
are cutting their health benefits, and major layoffs are
coming. The European economic boom is going to
come at America's expense.

RM: Is there any way we can forestall that or minimize the
problem?

AK: The only way around it would be politically risky and
require a radical reorganization of our political and
economic rules. And that only happens when there are
no alternatives left. I don't see it coming without major
social upheaval in this country. Now, if you asked me
tomorrow and I was in a better mood, I might have a
more optimistic outlook. But it's hard to see much hope
right now.

~

Timothy Leary, so-called father of LSD, is now back on
the lecture circuit but not commanding the kind of attention
he once did. Whatever else one might think about him, he
continues to proselytize for his beliefs despite criticism and
dismissal by academic colleagues.

Leary came to prominence at the same time as the late
Marshall McLuhan, and both of them scandalized their
academic colleagues. McLuhan once enraged an audience of
professors by responding to a critic, "You don't like my
ideas? I've got others." McLuhan cared little for the preten-
sions of the scholarly community. Several 1989 biographies
paint him as a loner, a rebel, ostracized by his peers and
accused of intolerably bad writing. His influence was so

pervasive that his name lent a new adjective (McLuhan-esque) and noun (McLuhanism) to the common language.

~

Arlo Guthrie is still performing the good old folk songs his father Woody made famous, bless their souls. **Eartha Kitt**, who had some choice words for Lyndon Johnson's wife Lady Bird (which reduced the ladybird to tears), can still manage a ninety-minute set and is much loved by the gay crowd. **Larry Bensky**, **Todd Gitlin**, **Michael Rossman**, these old radicals haven't left Berkeley yet. And **H. Rap Brown** just resurfaced as a Muslim fundamentalist, con-demning Salman Rushdie over *The Satanic Verses*.

~

Steve Diamond is the author of the nonfiction book *What the Trees Said*, detailing the lives of the Liberation News Service farmers at the commune in Montague, Massachu-setts, and the novel *Panama Red*, the adventures of a fic-tional marijuana dealer. Born in Panama City in 1946, he grew up there and in Miami with journalist parents who published an international magazine for Latin-American tourists. He masterminded the Beatles' *Magical Mystery Tour* New York premier as a benefit for Liberation News Service and with Marshall Bloom purchased the LNS farm in Montague. Today he lives in Santa Barbara.

RM: Whatever happened to Steve Diamond?
SD: Well, I'm happy living in Santa Barbara and just mak-ing arrangements for the Christmas holiday visit from my daughters.
RM: What's happening with you now, what are your major concerns? I've described you as the genius who got us the Beatles benefit and bought the farm.
SD: After leaving the farm, then, here's my story. Following some discord at the farm, I devoted my life to a spiritual

trip. Living next to nature, I discovered the truth of that
line in *Zen and the Art of Motorcycle Maintenance*, "The
real cycle you're working on is the cycle called yourself." You find out what kind of person you are. You
have to change, to grow, to heal. Change your way of
thinking—think globally and act locally. Out here in
Santa Barbara I've been active in the New Age flowering ever since the Harmonic Convergence on August
17, 1987.

RM: I remember that one. What effect did it have?

SD: It had repercussions all around the world. Within the
month of September, Reagan announced that Gorba-
chev was going to come to Washington. And the world
has been rapidly moving to harmonize ever since. This
is the most important development in our lifetimes. It's
the flowering of the seeds we planted in the 1960s.
They're actually talking about reducing nuclear weapons. For three years a meditation group here has been
meeting once a week, sending beams of light to earth.
Their ohmmmmms represent the sound of the universe.
We're experiencing an amazing burst of New Age activity. Seems like every small town in America has an
organic food store, a mystical bookstore.

RM: In Carmel there are three or four of them.

SD: Astrology has never been so popular. In the Age of
Aquarius, everybody's into it, even the president and his
wife. What you ought to do, Raymond, is the biography
of Sydney Omarr. He has a giant following, and maybe
he'd reveal all the secrets of the stars. If somebody
wrote a great biography of him, it would sell.

RM: Maybe, but in New York the major publishers would
probably pooh-pooh astrology and not take it seriously.
What are you working on now?

SD: I'm working on a booklet about UFOs. It's a pretty far-
out story.

RM: I'd like to hear it.

SD: OK, you should know this because it's true. UFOs
really did crash in this country in the 1940s. The gov-

ernment kept it under wraps so only a small body of
people were aware of it. They studied them for the next
twenty years into the 1960s, but couldn't figure them
out. Meanwhile, there were many more sightings at
military installations, which the public didn't hear
about. In 1972 Nixon went to China and took along a
videotape of UFO activity and exchanged notes with
the Chinese. They formed a joint team to study the
phenomena. This is the first time humanity has been
contending with alien forces among us. We're heading
for a future time of a world government.

RM: We do seem to be getting along better.

SD: Listen—all of this has happened before. It's just that
the human race can't remember it. The Hindus believe
that individual humans have many incarnations. Each
time you're here in the body, you become a bit more
purified through suffering until you're pure enough in
spirit to move onto the next higher plane of existence
toward the Godhead, closer and closer to the source of
the force. Could it be that humankind itself has several
lifetimes? And in each of these, humanity comes closer
to purification? Is there still time enough for us to live
in harmony with Mother Earth?

Of all the original fellows of the Fellowship of
Religious Youth, I'm the only one who considers himself religious still. Spiritualism is very big in Santa
Barbara. I'm also working for a vocational rehabilita-
tion agency, which trains people for new jobs. You'd
love doing this work. It's just like the sixties. I get on
the phone, talk to the employers, match up their needs
with those of my clients. I put people together. It's
satisfying.

~

Mitchell Danielson, described as a wild eighteen-year-old
motorcyclist from Oregon traveling around the world on
second-class freighters, is today the marketing director for
Esprit fashions in San Francisco, as yuppie and upscale an

enterprise as you'll find anywhere. "I make plenty of money," he said in 1989, "but it's lonely in city life. I know a lot of people, but real friends are rare." Twenty years after his initial tour of India on dusty back roads, Mitchell still visits there occasionally—via airplane, for a week in a comfy hotel, natch. That's the difference between being twenty and forty. When you're older you can't stand the pain and discomfort you cheerfully put up with as a lad, and you simply won't take the same chances with life.

~

Jane Fonda just got back from Asia too, and in a tired frame of mind. "Please, no interviews," she pleaded. "There's nothing left in me to say. I'm completely exhausted. I need some time off." Yet what she's been saying has reached so far and wide as to need no amplification here.

Her latest book is a fitness guide for pregnant women, and she says that she wishes she'd had such a book when she was having her own children, Vanessa (by film director Roger Vadim) and Troy (by Tom Hayden). She is remarkable in every way, a woman who has achieved world-class success in not one but five or six careers—actress, political leader and peace activist, fitness expert, author, namesake and entrepreneur of health centers, famous daughter, sister, mother.

The breakup of her marriage to Hayden is something neither will discuss publicly, but in the general scheme of things you can be sure the gossip rags and tell-all columnists will have plenty to say. By the time you read this, each may be publicly loving someone else. It's no life for the faint of heart. They'll both be dead before the whole truth comes out.

~

Roger Rappaport is described in *Famous Long Ago* as the kindly editor of the *Michigan Daily* student newspaper who provided housing and comfort to Bloom, Bala-Bala, and myself after we left the U.S. Student Press Association.

Always a staunch supporter of LNS and press freedoms, he is today a staff writer and travel editor at the *Oakland Tribune*.

RM: In *Famous Long Ago*, Roger, you were described as a good guy and ally. How have you been?

RR: Great. Where are you these days?

RM: In southern California, writing my new book and pursuing movie producers. After you talk to them, you have to take a shower.

RR: They are real fly-by-night people, everybody says so, but it may sound worse than it really is. I've never tried to actually write a script, although I've had some of my work optioned. There must be something wrong with me that I don't have the drive. I feel like I'm the only writer who doesn't have this burning ambition to sell a script tomorrow. I mean, I love going to L.A. and I know it's lucrative, but I hear so much bitching and moaning from other writers.

RM: Oh yeah, it's even worse than the book trade. You did have several books published, didn't you?

RR: Recently I've been doing a series of travel books. The latest one is about Asia, there's one about California, and one about traveling around the world. They're called *22 Days in Asia*, *22 Days in California*, and *22 Days Around the World*.

RM: So it's the *22 Days Series*.

RR: Yes, published by John Muir Publications; they're really nice people to work with.

RM: I did a book about Asia once, quite different. It was footloose, stoned wanderings. And you're still working at the *Oakland Tribune*?

RR: Yes, as travel editor and staff writer. I also do some freelancing, a little bit of magazine work, but my job is on the staff, working with the editors. I'm still living in Berkeley and have two kids.

RM: So what do you see has happened to our generation? Do you have any philosophical insights? Did our generation really improve America, or is the whole thing going down the tubes?

RR: That's a good question. You know, as it gets further and further away in time, there's a tendency toward trashing a lot of the things that we did when we were young. It starts out as satire, making fun of the flower children or hippies. Teachers tell the kids what went on then, the information gets dated. But we have a much better handle on it now. Things were happening much faster then. Now, things may be regressing. People are much more conservative, not taking risks anymore. We took a lot of chances back then. I think a lot of the things we predicted would happen have happened. But what comes home is what a small minority we were, even then.

RM: It's interesting that you said that. We made a big noise and a big media presence, but actually most people our age weren't politically active at the time. We took chances, for sure. Burn your draft card, you could go to jail. I think it's fair to say our lives were on the line. Those of us who were active were very vocal and bright, but the majority were just trudging off to the factory or the army.

RR: You're still taking a lot of chances, I think.

RM: The only chance I take is that I've never had a job. Which means my income goes to wild extremes. That's the nature of being a freelance writer; it's the most insecure thing on earth unless you happen to have a bestseller. But I've never starved. I've always had a support network around me.

RR: The only people who get credit for taking chances these days are the entrepreneurs, but they are still playing within the Establishment.

～

Steve d'Arazien, another journalistic colleague, followed his political instincts to Washington and a succession of jobs with the federal government ranging from press secretary to a Congressman to his current post writing for the Center for Disease Control in Atlanta. "Just dropped Howard Zinn a note since he is doing something for the Abbie Hoffman Memorial, which is admirable," Steve writes in a letter. "And Jeff Kaliss, never a movement type, called me at CDC to say he'd quit his job and was now an entertainment writer. Well, I guess I understand why one would quit a job with the government, since I have one myself (but I have independence and a relatively good salary and perhaps even a future). I'd like to write a novel about those times [the sixties] but I can't do it while in the employ of CDC. I work and come home tired, get to bed early, and besides that, what I do at work is—yep, write. I may wait until I'm retired, or forget it."

~

Howard Zinn is one of the best-known radical historians in the United States, a longtime professor of history at Boston University, and author of many books. He was one of our great supporters during the civil rights, antiwar, and student uprising days of the 1960s. In *Famous Long Ago*, he is quoted with a telegram to LNS sent from North Vietnam, where he visited to represent the U.S. peace movement. He and his wife, Roslyn, still live in the Boston area.

HZ: Your book is a good idea. About five years ago I was saying to Ros it would be a good idea to write a book about where are they now. I had this romantic notion that I'd travel around the country seeing old friends, find out how they're doing. Seems that you're doing something like that.

RM: Exactly, and I've really enjoyed the traveling. Of course I do come to the Boston area at least once a year anyway to check up on my mother, who still lives in Lawrence.

HZ: Just leaving Lawrence made you a success.

RM: Yes, but my mother never understood why I wanted to

be a writer and a radical. She would have preferred that I had a regular paycheck.

HZ: That's how most mothers are.

RM: All these years I've continued to have a great admiration for your work. I've read your books and your articles here and there. You're no longer at Boston University, however, is that right?

HZ: Right. I quit BU about a year ago, and I'm very happy about that. I was there for twenty-four years.

RM: You're a living legend there.

HZ: It was a long time, and I made a quick decision. It wasn't that I didn't like teaching. I was still loving my teaching and had four hundred students in my class, but you know how you get tired of doing something even if it's really good? You've been doing something a long time and you really need a break. I needed to be free. I would come home from teaching a three-hour class and I was exhausted. I wanted to have more time to write. Some years ago I began to write plays.

RM: I didn't know that. Have they been produced?

HZ: Yes, two have been produced. Just after the Vietnam War ended, I wrote a play about Emma Goldman.

RM: One of my heroines.

HZ: And one of mine. The play was produced in New York, then it was done in Boston, had a long run in Boston, a few years ago it was revived in New York, then in London. It's going to be done in Tokyo next spring.

RM: What's the title?

HZ: *Emma.* So I got sort of bitten by the bug. It was exciting and a lot of fun. There's something especially satisfying about doing something for the theater. You know how hard it is to write a book? Well, it's even harder to do a play.

RM: Will they send you to Japan for the opening?

HZ: Yes, it's unbelievable how the Japanese love American writers.

RM: Oh, I know, they've treated me very well.

HZ: You've been there?

RM: Yes, I have a publisher in Tokyo and some of my books have done better there than in the U.S. Did you say you'd written another play?

HZ: Yes, my second play was produced in New York and then Connecticut, and I just got a letter from a company in Boulder, Colorado, who wants to do it next summer. I love writing for the theater. It's one of the reasons I quit teaching, to have more time to write the things I like instead of writing history books. But *The People's History of the United States* did very well.

RM: I recently saw it featured in a bookstore front window in Santa Monica.

HZ: A Harper & Row editor told me it's one of the very few books which sells more each year than the year before. Since 1981, it's sold about 150,000 copies, or roughly 20,000 a year now, and it has not diminished. Every year I think my next royalty check is going to be for about $7.29, because most of my other books give me royalty checks like that.

RM: *The People's History* is a modern classic.

HZ: Thank you. It's done so well, and it's a nice feeling to get mail about the book, letters from the readers. But I really want to write different stuff. I'd like to write for the movies. Fun things.

RM: It sounds like you're enjoying life.

HZ: I feel liberated, gone from BU.

RM: You must have run into controversies with [conservative BU president] John Silber.

HZ: Oh, God, it was absolute total war. He hated me. Lots of people politically disagreed with me, but Silber actively hated me. He's a very paranoid, very smart man, very tough. The faculty twice voted to recommend to the trustees that they dismiss him, but he wasn't deterred by that. He's strong; he built himself a little military junta in charge of the university.

RM: In the years that I edited the *BU News*, we were very idealistic, we thought we were winning. We ousted [president] Harold Case, we kicked the ROTC off campus, we overturned the birth control laws, we firmly prevented them from censoring that paper.

HZ: Those were great years. I still have a *BU News* cover from that era on my office wall. And Ros still uses the Total Loss Farm book [*Home Comfort*] all the time; it's her favorite cookbook.

RM: Total Loss has had an incredible staying power. Most of the sixties communes didn't. They broke apart or turned into a more conventional arrangement.

HZ: What are you finding about what people are doing?

RM: The truth is, my generation, people turning forty or so, are leading more ordinary lives than we used to. Most of us just couldn't keep it up. People get married, have children, have responsibilities, they don't have the same energy they had when they were twenty-two years old and rioting in the street. There's nothing wrong with that, it's just not very dramatic.

HZ: Well, the encouraging thing is that while a lot of these people in their forties may have settled down, there is a whole new generation of young people coming forth. Ros and I went to a memorial service yesterday for the Jesuit priests who were killed in El Salvador; there were about four hundred people there and we looked around and we didn't know anybody there. And we thought, that's a good sign. They were all new faces and mostly young people. There are young kids all over the country active on nuclear power issues, Central America, Rocky Flats.

RM: I'm glad to hear it. I don't know if it's a sweeping trend or what.

HZ: It's not sweeping yet, but it's growing. I'm optimistic for the future.

~

Allen Ginsberg grew up and became our national poet laureate unofficially crowned. We were proud to publish his long poem *These States* in LNS January 29, 1968:

> *These are the names of the companies that have made money from Chinese war . . .*

These are the corporations who have profited
   merchandising skinburning phosphorous or shells
   fragmented into thousands of flesh-piercing
   needles . . .
and these are the names of the generals & captains of
   military, who now thus work for wargoods
   manufacturers . . .

And so forth. Allen invited Marshall and me to his farm
in Cherry Valley, New York, where he lived with Peter Or-
lovsky and sometimes Gregory Corso and was visited by his
father, Louis, who was also a poet, although more conventional. And, while he was always a strong force for progressive politics, Allen also served us as a kindly, avuncular role
model of gayness when few were available. The first really
comprehensive biography of Ginsberg came out in 1989,
and it's sexually explicit, which is phenomenal in itself for a
literary work about a living writer.

The only other publicly gay writer I can recall from
those years was Paul Goodman, author of *Growing up Ab-
surd*, who was married and had a family and lived part-time
on a farm in New Hampshire not far from our place in
Vermont. But Paul didn't make an issue of his sexuality; it
was something known to the cognoscenti but not wildly
celebrated in the Ginsberg fashion.

The trademark Allen Ginsberg hair and beard, once
considered so outrageous, are gone, and today's poet looks
rather like a portly college professor. Ginsberg may never be
formally recognized with any type of national arts medal,
yet he is arguably the best-known poet in the land.

~

Marlene Hersch worked with photographer Robert Map-
plethorpe but died shortly before he did, after suffering a
toxic reaction to an antibiotic prescribed for a simple uri-
nary infection. She was in her early thirties. None of her
friends could believe it. She was young and full of life and

felled by a million-to-one freak accident of modern medicine. We're all on thin ice. An hour could be forever.

~

Numerous others, who have asked to remain anonymous here, came down with HIV infection or full-blown AIDS symptoms, and some have already died. We wait and pray for the others.

~

Eric Utne abandoned psychedelic drugs after becoming a devotee of guru Michio Kuchi and founding the magazine *New Age Journal*. Today, he publishes the *Utne Reader*, which in May 1990 hosted a Minneapolis conference where the Network of the Alternative Student Press announced the formation of "New Liberation News Service." Utne means "far out" in Norwegian.

~

Allen Young was a "straight" journalist, working for such publications as the *Washington Post* and the *Christian Science Monitor*, when he joined forces with Marshall Bloom and me at Liberation News Service in Washington, D.C. He later sided with the New York LNS people in our internecine quarrel and went on working for LNS in New York after Bloom, et al., had moved to the country commune. He left LNS in 1973 to form a commune of his own with other gay men in western Massachusetts and has continued to write and publish. Since we had been enemies, or at least members of rival camps, I was a bit unsure of what kind of reception to expect from Allen, but he was cordial and glad to talk about the old and current days.

RM: How have you been?
AY: Just fine. I hoped I'd see you at the farm reunion.

RM: I've enjoyed reading some of your contributions to gay history.

AY: Yes, I did three anthologies with the lesbian writer Carla Jay and a special report on gays under the Cuban revolution.

RM: I read your piece on gays in Cuba. It was a tough one for me too, but as you know I was never very political.

AY: Last I heard you had a bookstore in Carmel.

RM: Actually the bookstore was in Seattle, and we had a small-press publishing operation.

AY: I had a small-press publishing company too, but it's been somewhat disastrous. It's a tough way to make money. I sit around at my job and read ads that say, "Clip this coupon and become a freelance writer." But I know I need the job.

RM: What kind of job is it?

AY: Right now I'm the director of public relations for the local hospital.

RM: Well, that sounds great. There was a time twenty years ago when if we even heard the term *public relations* . . .

AY: We'd throw up!

RM: Right. But if you're representing something you believe in, it's fine.

AY: I also worked for the local daily newspaper, the *Athol Daily News*.

RM: So what are you doing these days, what is your philosophy of life?

AY: As a matter of fact, and not to feed your ego, but there's a wonderful sentence near the end of *Famous Long Ago* where you say, "I don't believe in anything but trees." And I pay attention to trees, that's my credo.

RM: Well, I heard you'd moved to the country.

AY: Really, I remember that line so much. The most recent thing I did, and probably closest to my heart, is joining the board of directors of our local conservation land trust. And I was the chairman of the zoning board of appeals.

RM: Do you live in a communal situation today?

AY: No, not exactly. My neighbors and I have an agreement about publicity; we don't want to publicize this place.

RM: We don't have to even mention the name of the town.

AY: Oh, I'm not that worried. Basically I came here with a group of gay men, and we have modified our arrangement over the years. We now have four houses on what used to be one piece of land, which was later subdivided. It's not entirely different from Packer's Corners [Total Loss Farm], although the evolution was a little different.

RM: Well, in their case also, some individuals bought pieces of the land and built homes, and they had to own the land privately in order to get bank loans.

AY: I feel particularly good about moving to the country. I moved here in 1973, five years after "the guns of August" [the 1968 war within LNS]. Five years today doesn't seem like much. But within a very short period of time, Sam Lovejoy toppled the nuclear tower and I became involved in the antinuke movement. At that time George [Cavalletto] and Sheila [Ryan] became rabid pro-Palestinian activists while I looked a little more at the Israeli side. I made peace with my situation.

RM: I remember thinking about that time, "Allen must have come around to our point of view. He moved to western Massachusetts, and he's gay, and I'm all of that."

AY: Well, it still bothers me to read your description of me in *Famous Long Ago*, "Allen Young was in Bulgaria at some kind of conference when we heisted the presses." That book had a real influence in its time, and they still use it in colleges as a history of the 1960s, I think.

RM: Oh God, I'll never live it down. Maybe a few places, yes. I've been asked to speak to classes studying the 1960s who read the book as one of their texts.

AY: Have you spoken to George and Sheila yet?

RM: No, and I probably won't. I didn't really know them, whereas we were friends and we worked together.

AY: Are you still with your Japanese-American boyfriend?

RM: Oh, yes, we're married more than eight years.

AY: I have a boyfriend too; we've been together for years and we spend the weekends together, but we don't live together.

~

Susan Dalsimer, the extraordinary editor who, as Susan Stern, produced counterculture books by Ed Sanders, Paul Williams, Rudolph Wurlitzer, myself, and many others, is now the chief story editor for Lorimar Productions (TV and movies) in New York. She married a doctor, had two children, and is "extremely happy and doing very well" and promised to tell all, as long as I "don't put it in the book."

~

Abe Peck, editor of the underground *Chicago Seed* in the days of LNS, wrote a book of his own about what happened to the '60s alternative-media folks, *Uncovering the Sixties*, and a good book it is. He's now a professor at the Medill School of Journalism at Northwestern University, which to my knowledge makes him the only underground editor to rise to a position of scholarly respectability. However, all the old LNS files and published issues have been carefully enshrined in university libraries, principally at Yale and Amherst College. And I'm sure these artifacts are being studied by earnest doctoral candidates as we speak. One graduate student at the University of Massachusetts, earning a master's degree in communications, sent me a paper he wrote about my early books, in which he claimed they all have three-word titles (*Famous Long Ago, Total Loss Farm, Return to Sender*, etc.) because I was raised as a Catholic kid to worship the Holy Trinity!

~

Dan Riley, radical student editor at the University of Hartford, resurfaced in Thousand Oaks, California, cushy suburb of L.A., where he wrote and self-published *The Red Sox*

Reader, a lively collection of essays on the Boston Red Sox by famous authors such as Roger Angell, Thomas Boswell, Red Smith, George Will, and John Updike (who contributed his classic essay on the last day that Ted Williams played at Fenway Park, "Hub Fans Bid Kid Adieu"). Now in its third printing, the book was so successful that Dan gave up his job at a computer company and authored another, completely different, book called *The Diary of Jesus H. Christ*, purported to be journal entries of Christ in heaven. Some Catholics in Boston were not amused.

~

Jesse Kornbluth is the author of *Notes from the New Underground*, an original contributor to LNS, and currently a contributing editor and staff writer for *Vanity Fair* magazine. His work has appeared in many periodicals, and his books and screenplays have succeeded to the extent that he is one of New York's best-known writers.

RM: I just received a catalog in which they're selling out-of-print copies of your old book *Notes from the New Underground*.

JK: I hope they're selling for a dollar ninety-five.

RM: No, Jesse, twenty-five bucks a copy.

JK: Really? Are they selling *Famous Long Ago* too?

RM: No, but they offer my screenplay *Between Two Moons*, my least successful and most imponderable book, for that price. It makes me feel old.

JK: Raymond, we're not having any old age. What have you learned in researching your new book?

RM: It's not amazing, but I've learned that the vast majority of people who may have been quite wild and crazy in the sixties did retire to rather ordinary lives. And I guess that's only to be expected.

JK: Listen, I went to my fifth Harvard reunion and swore I'd never go back. In only five years, they'd already turned into their fathers.

RM: I see your byline everywhere.

JK: Well, you can't see it everywhere. I'm only allowed to write for *Vanity Fair* and twice a year for the *New York Times.*

RM: Didn't I see something of yours in *Condé Nast Traveler* magazine recently?

JK: You're right. It's an exception, but the only reason I can write for the *Traveler* is it's being edited by the husband of the woman who runs *Vanity Fair.* It's a very tight thing.

RM: There are writers who would die for that arrangement.

JK: Oh, hey, I'm not complaining. You can say, "The Kornbluths are living high above their means on Central Park West." But it takes a lot of tap dancing.

RM: You're very good at it.

JK: I'm a triple Capricorn. If I can't be good at it, who can? I'm just a person who didn't like outhouses. It's very simple; it's all negative propulsion in my case. I know very well how unadaptable I am. This afternoon I saw Jerry Lefcourt—he was the Black Panther lawyer and Abbie Hoffman's lawyer—and he and I are involved in the same struggle, which is the repeal of the racketeering law, which is unbelievably unconstitutional. I'm writing a book about Michael Milliken, and I said to him, "Michael, twenty years ago I was having the same conversations, but I never thought I'd have them with people in suits, people with money."

RM: What kind of conversation?

JK: Conversations about liberty.

RM: Do you have a contract for this book on Milliken?

JK: Yes, with Random House. It's a book about the eighties. We're all involved in the same struggle for human freedom and dignity. The difference between then and now is just that now we're smart enough not to put a label on it in dull political parties. In every generation there's always someone who is chosen to be the victim. In the sixties it was the Vietnam protestors and blacks, in the seventies it was someone else, in the late eighties it turns out to be investment bankers. It's unusual that these are the sort of people we started out hating and now find ourselves defending. It's vastly more sophisticated now.

RM: When I think back, I never hated bankers, I never called police "pigs." I just wasn't that militant.

JK: I think of a lot of that period as the lost years, from 1969 to '74 or '75, when the situation was generally unfavorable and we were really struggling. I'm still struggling, but I'm struggling in a higher tax bracket.

RM: Which of your books are still in print? You wrote that book with the CEO of the Pepsi corporation.

JK: The Pepsi book is known in my agent's office as the book that would not die. It's still paying royalties. More interesting to me is a book called *Pre-Pop Warhol*, published by Random House, about Andy Warhol's early life. It's a complete projection of him as an outsider with his nose pressed against the glass, and if there's anything I understand, it's that. It's Andy as a successful commercial artist from 1949 to 1959, and it was immensely pleasurable to do. I'm now writing the ABC television movie about Leona Helmsley.

RM: And you have two kids?

JK: Two stepchildren, nine and five years old. The first time I was married, the wedding cost five hundred thousand dollars. I could have made a movie for that.

RM: Jesse, it's so much fun to talk to you.

JK: Raymond, conversation is our game. The real drag is I have to seduce people one at a time. It would be so much more efficient to talk to groups.

RM: Well, every person is different. I'm just awash in memories of the old days.

JK: New York is on the verge of being 1973 all over again.

RM: Why do you say that?

JK: The fiscal crisis, gloom and doom, the party's over, it's fashionable to be pessimistic.

RM: People say New York is like a Third World country these days.

JK: It's not enough of a Third World country, that's the problem.

RM: It's Third World in appearance, but twenty-first century in expense.

~

Craig Spratt, who may have had the distinction of being the craziest and wooliest of our bunch at LNS, is now a lawyer with a starched-shirt Boston firm representing large insurance interests. It figures, given the ironic nature of things in general. Craig is mentioned often in *Famous Long Ago*, "as often as not underfoot," a manic and very talented writer whose essays like "Sir John the Sincere" (a pornographic epic) became legendary LNS copy. The *San Francisco Oracle* used splashy purple graphics to illustrate Craig's timeless creations. He was also a tireless and devoted worker who stuck with LNS while many others collapsed.

He married and had a daughter, Gretchen, now a college student, and I suppose marriage and children will put the fear of God in any young man. Most of us did have kids in the last two decades, and people with children are categorically different from those without.

There is a tendency to invest one's energy, hope, money, and love in the offspring. To some extent, your own life begins to end when the baby comes out. We pass the baton. SDS had a twentieth-anniversary reunion in 1988, and participants each wrote a paragraph or two about how their own lives had evolved in the time between. Many of them mentioned their children first, as their greatest accomplishments.

~

Bill Ayres and **Bernardine Dohrn** have three kids, Jayd, Malik, and Chesa. "They give our lives all the shape and hope we need," Bill wrote. Honey Williams described herself first as "the mother of Sarah Hope Williams, age 5," second as "an aging hippie driving her tractor and considering what to do next after retiring from corporate life at 40." Steve Johnson rated marriage and the birth of his child as highlights of his life and quoted a favorite saying, "When raising children, the most important thing is to give them self-confidence. To do this, remember, 'Always support, never compare.'"

~

Peter Simon is a well-known photographer whose books of pictures and text have been quite successful. He is the son of the late Richard Simon, cofounder of Simon & Schuster publishers, and Andrea Simon, and brother of singers Carly and Joanna Simon. The illustrious clan hails from Riverdale, New York, and I first met Peter at Boston University, where he was the photo editor of the *BU News* during my stint as editor in chief. He was also active in Liberation News Service, helped us buy Total Loss Farm, and himself bought a share in the farm next door to us, Tree Frog Farm. Peter is now married and ensconced year-round at Gay Head, Martha's Vineyard.

RM: Are you working on a book?

PS: Actually, I put together a retrospective photography book about my life, or I've been toying with the idea. As you know, I've kept a journal almost all of my life, although not as much lately, and I put together a lengthy proposal, which included a lot about you.

RM: I'm flattered.

PS: Well, every publisher I brought it to said, "Hey, this is interesting, but I'll need to see a couple of chapters." And by the time I got around to writing them, April arrived and that's when I get really busy, so I haven't gotten to the writing.

RM: You're busy in April doing photography?

PS: Yes, ninety percent of it here on Martha's Vineyard. What brings in the most money is weddings and family portraits. They're all done in a real—informal—style.

RM: Sounds like you've developed your own style.

PS: Yes, and I'm very well known around here. It's like being a big fish in a small pond.

RM: The last time I saw you was at that reunion party at Tree Frog in 1980, wasn't it?

PS: No, I remember very clearly the last time was during the 1980 World Series with the Phillies. We watched it on TV at my house, and I took a picture of you for your baseball book.

RM: I still have the picture.

PS: I feel guilty I haven't kept in touch.

RM: I feel the same way! Tell me what your concerns are nowadays, how you look at our generation.

PS: Well, during the 1960s and 1970s you and Ram Dass exerted a lot of influence on me, and that influence was good, but I think a lot of people screwed up their lives with all the drugs and dropping out. I have a lot of friends like _____ who still haven't gotten it together. If I hadn't gone through all those changes, I'd be like those straighter people in New York City making a lot more money. I never really have achieved the level of success I could have, but my life is much healthier and more sane.

    Around '81 or '82 I started having these anxiety attacks. I hated flying. Couldn't bear it. It was a kind of agoraphobia, you know, I was afraid to leave home. I turned into a deejay, spinning records at dance clubs both here in Martha's Vineyard and in New York until I hurt my ears. I started hearing high-pitched ringing sounds; it was horrible at first, but it's much less now. I guess you could say I'm a casualty of the rock generation. I'm still into the music, but I don't listen to it as loudly.

RM: What about your books? Which ones are still in print?

PS: *Reggae Bloodlines*, that I did with Steve Davis, is still in print, and one called *Playing in the Band*, that was about the Grateful Dead. And I'm publishing an annual calendar on Martha's Vineyard that's been very successful. And ten years ago I did a book called *On the Vineyard* with my photos and texts by some of the real famous authors who live here—you know, Updike and Styron and so forth. That one is out of print but people are always asking me for a copy, saying they'll pay a hundred dollars for a copy even. So I've decided to put out a new edition next year, call it *On the Vineyard, Volume 2*. I'm sure it will sell.

RM: What do you call your publishing company?

PS: Simon Press. In a smaller way, I guess you could say I'm following in my father's footsteps.

~

Jeff Nightbyrd, who was known as Jeff Shero when he edited *The Rat* newspaper in New York, cautioned our generation about health in his SDS reunion report. "What's on my mind is heart attacks," he wrote. "A friend from the underground paper in Madison had a massive coronary last week. Too many cigarettes, too much sitting behind a desk, editing. His forty-five-year-old heart didn't take kindly to the weekly tennis game.

"I watched too many friends embrace middle age in the sedentary style of our parents' generation. Maybe giving up on your body reflects a certain resignation about life? Of course, some suffer from simple bad luck or genetics. But, if you're not fit, it's hard to be enthusiastic, it's damn hard to be active, and your disposition tends to be a little sour. I tell New Age types, thirty minutes of exericise is worth two weeks of affirmations."

~

Walter Bowart is a truly mythological character out of the underground. With the late Allen Katzman, he founded and edited New York's *East Village Other* newspaper, an alternative to the *Village Voice*, which thrived in the '60s. In *Famous Long Ago*, he is described as wearing an Indian headdress to the big organizational meeting of LNS held in Washington in conjunction with the March on Washington, in October 1968. Since then, he has informed me it was no Indian headdress but a particular kind of hat. When last heard from he was editing *Palm Springs Life* magazine, a journal of affluent living, but he left Palm Springs and apparently disappeared into the hills of New Mexico. Six months of tracing and postal searches found him in a place called Chokonen Sanctuary in Paradise, Arizona, and this interview was conducted by phone from the lobby of the Douglas Hotel in Douglas, Arizona.

RM: Walter, where are you and how are you?

WB: I'm fine; I'm down on the Mexican border. Sorry it took me so long to answer your letters. I'm doing my life plan. My retirement plan, the thing I've been aiming at since I left New York and came here. I'm building a resort in the mountains, a hundred acres surrounded by national forest in a rare ecological area called the Chiricahua Mountains.

RM: Sounds far out.

WB: Oh, it's far out all right. My market is birdwatchers, naturalists, environmentalists. Hey, if I'm in your book, I hope I ain't wearing no Indian headdress. The Indians up here are extinct.

RM: Don't worry about it. Where exactly is Paradise, Arizona?

WB: Near Tombstone and Bisbee. You'll have to come out for a visit. Tombstone's the town too tough to die, Bisbee the town too high to care, and Paradise no town at all.

RM: Well, you sound good. What else is happening?

WB: Well, I just turned fifty and right away joined the AARP [American Association of Retired Persons]. Then I found out it's owned by an insurance company. So I've got to start a new organization, the AARRP.

RM: AARRP?

WB: American Association of Retired *Radical* Persons.

RM: I can't wait till I'm old enough to join.

WB: The insurance companies are screwing everybody up. You know, they won't even let you die without a medical card. I buried both my parents in Palm Springs. My father died there, and his last words to me were, "Thank you very much." I've been trying to get my stuff published for over a year now, a finished novel which Bob Gover [author of *The Hundred Dollar Misunderstanding*] loved and wrote a lengthy recommendation on, and some nonfiction ideas. Either I've lost the knack or I'm on some kind of blacklist. Now I'm working on an autobiographical novel called *Affluenza*, about my life with Peggy Mellon Hitchcock.

RM: Wasn't she your first wife?

WB: Right. I used to be called the oldest hippie. I was born in 1939, when Hitler invaded Poland. The big thing that got me over hippiedom was when I married the Mellon bank. There was this headline in Suzy's column in the *New York Daily News* or the *Post*, I can't remember which, "Artist/Intellectual, Ex-Hippie, Marries Peggy Mellon." Peggy and I were living in a tepee in Arizona in 1968, but I lost my hippie credentials. Then I moved to Aspen, Colorado, for four years. I was the editor of the *Aspen Daily News* and replaced Hunter S. Thompson on a sheriff's committee. Some people thought I *was* Hunter S. Thompson.

RM: Then you had a book out, right?

WB: Yes, my book on the CIA, *Operation Mind Control*, was published by Dell in 1978. I did ninety-eight radio and TV interviews in thirty cities and the book did very well, but the CIA went around buying up all the copies. That's my assumption, anyway. You couldn't find the book anywhere. It happened in France, Holland, Britain. One British bookseller said that a well-known CIA operative came in and ordered fifty copies. At the same time, other books used the same evidence I did but didn't reach the same conclusions. I coined the terms *cryptocrat* and *cryptocracy*, damaging propaganda terms. I predicted the arms-Contra deal. The book was being sold underground in a Xerox copy version in the Soviet Union.

I also revealed that Timothy Leary was getting his drugs from the CIA. He admitted it. I'm working on a book called *Holy Acid Wars and Other Crusades of the '60s*. I still feel a person has the right to alter his own consciousness, although I can see how people get badly hooked on booze and pot and so forth. I never tried crack. I testified for the Senate subcommittee on drugs in 1966, and I'd love to do an unauthorized biography on Leary. He's like a double agent.

I can't divorce my politics from my spirituality. In my FBI file, they said, "He's not a subversive, but a dangerous free thinker." Can you believe that coming from a government founded by Thomas Jefferson? But you can still change public opinion by writing a book.

RM: Yes, but how have you been supporting yourself?

WB: With real estate. I accumulated a lot of it when Peggy and I were together. Recently I sold my house in Port Townsend, Washington, and I'm getting ready to sell my place in California. I sold my ex-wife some of my one hundred acres here, and the money allows me to build. I'm planning to build twenty or twenty-five cabins out here, hire a gourmet chef, and have a gala opening.

RM: And your family?

WB: My son, J.J., is just starting kindergarten. Peggy and I have two daughters away at school, but last year was wonderful in that I got to see them frequently. Sophia's eighteen. She hates the negative reinforcement system of grading at her college and will probably change schools next year. Nuri is sixteen. She and six other students were recently busted running naked around the campus in the rain. I'm gonna frame the letter the dean of protocol sent me.

RM: You sound happy down there.

WB: Yeah, but it's wild. Everybody's armed!

～

Danny Schechter, who was with Marshall Bloom at the London School of Economics in the pre-LNS days and operated our London office, later became a top radio news director at WBCN in Boston, moved to New York for a stint with Ted Turner's Cable News Network, and is now "inside the news machine at ABC News. The Big Time!? '20/20' producer making the long march through the institutions we used to talk about. . . . I have not recanted. Still having second thoughts, third thoughts, schemes and dreams and more."

~

God help us,
refugees in winter dress
skating home on thin ice
from the Apocalypse
　　　　　—Verandah

~

Mel Lyman, where are you? He was the inspiration of the Boston underground paper *AVATAR* and object of passionate adoration and equally intense hatred from different camps. He grew amazingly strong pot at Fort Hill, a neighborhood commune in the middle of the ghetto in Roxbury, Massachusetts. Jim Kweskin and his Jug Band put out popular recordings and turned their royalties over to Mel. At least one major film, Antonioni's *Zabriskie Point*, was made with Lyman family stalwarts as actors. The whole group vanished but were reported to be in the Los Angeles area as recently as 1987, publishing an obscure magazine called *U and I*. Mel had married Jessie Benton, daughter of the great American painter Thomas Hart Benton, and they inherited some of his most famous works. Or so the stories go. So much of these '60s tales remain clouded, unclear, impossible to prove.

~

Tom Fels is an art curator in Bennington, Vermont, and **Michael Curry** a professor of geography at UCLA. Both were among the original residents of the Liberation News Service farm in Montague, Massachusetts, and Tom has acted as a kind of informal historian of that group, while Michael is one of the trustees named in the Fellowship of Religious Youth land trust deeded the farm by Marshall Bloom. This interview was conducted in the Huntley Hotel in Santa Monica while Tom was visiting California on assignment to restore antique photographs for the Getty Museum.

RM: I'm impressed with this new book, Tom, *O Say Can You See: American Photographs, 1839-1939*, published by MIT Press. By Thomas Weston Fels—I never knew you were a Weston. . . . It's a beautiful book. When did it come out?

TF: Just this year, in conjunction with a show at Bowdoin College in Maine. I acted as not only the writer and researcher but pretty much the publisher of the book.

RM: Even though it's published by MIT?

TF: There is still a life for the independent publisher, something I learned from you.

RM: When you say you were the publisher, you don't mean you actually had to put up the money for the printing?

TF: No, but I did all the physical coordinating. The interesting angle on this is that this is the 150th anniversary of photography, and there have been a lot of major shows at the National Gallery and the Met and so forth. But this show takes an alternative view of a different way of looking at photographs. It's locally written, locally printed and distributed.

RM: By local, you mean New England?

TF: Massachusetts. I say I'm publisher because it's part of my job. Museums, like many organizations, are overorganized, and when museums bounced back, which they did in the last ten or fifteen years, becoming major sources of entertainment for the public, they staffed themselves in such a way that every conceivable administrative angle is covered and nobody has any time to make exhibitions. So they hire outside people like me to do that. They said, "Do what you want with this private collection, perhaps the largest collection of early American photographs." I said, "With a show of this kind, why don't you have a book?" And they said yes and kind of looked the other way. So I wrote the book, picked the pictures, found a printer, and got a distributor.

RM: If you hadn't done it . . .

TF: If I hadn't done it, I don't think anyone would have minded, but it wouldn't have gotten done. It was an opening for private enterprise. My theory is that early American photography is important because it was the art of that culture, and this is the culture that pretty much dominated the modern era. Americans making photographs of the far West in 1850–1860 were laying the groundwork for the twentieth century.

RM: Did this work have its roots for you at the LNS farm in Montague?

TF: I came to the farm in Montague because I met Marshall at Amherst College, and we were not close friends but he was very meaningful to me. He was the first person who actually wrote about or expressed anything positive about what I had done. I became involved with some other people even as freshmen, and we organized a big conference on civil rights. Marshall wrote in the paper, look at what these freshmen have accomplished. It's really possible to have an idea and bring it to fruition. I was impressed that this great figure, the editor of the *Amherst Student*, respected what we'd done. Three or four years later, after I'd dropped out of college and was returning, the farm was just getting started and I moved in.

RM: So that's when we met, not in New York or Washington?

TF: Right. One difference between me and the others at the farm is that I'd grown up in the country and came from a progressive family. A lot of things the people at the farm touted were not new to me, and the reason I moved to the farm was I intended to write and draw and play music, and group living was a feasible way—almost the only feasible way in 1969 to do those things. I had no intention of going to graduate school at that time. I always saw the farm in terms of its illusions, whereas many people saw it as something to flee to because they hadn't experienced the freedom of a life where you could do what you wanted to do. I wanted to be effective in terms of the world. The reason I left the farm three or four years later was I didn't think they were being very effective at it. They were essentially another isolated community with its own vested interests. I moved back to the town where I grew up and knew people and thought I could be effective. I tried farming and carpentry to support my life and felt more a part of the actual world than staying in this highly idealistic community. Also, many of the people who interested me were no longer there; they'd moved away or died. The place changed.

RM: Montague was always completely different from our farm in Vermont.

TF: I never felt more comfortable than at Packer's Corners.

RM: It was always a nonprofit artists' corporation, whereas Montague was a bit confused. It's owned by the Fellowship of Religious Youth trust, but none of them are religious, young, or have lived at the farm in years. [Phone rings. It's Michael Curry in the lobby. Come on up, room 1202; room service brings wine and food.]

TF: You were talking about Montague. I don't agree with what Harvey Wasserman thinks should be done. He thinks it should be opened to a vast group of people voting on what to do with it.

RM: Democracy?

TF: But every worthwhile organization is run by a small group of people elected by a larger group of people. Having 150 people making a decision is not going to work. The fellowship should make provisions, elect new people if the old people don't want to serve or whatever, and go on to defend the original and basic values of that place. The fact that someone happens to have lived there for ten years doesn't mean that they own it. I lived in the same house for ten years, and I didn't own it.

RM: But land ownership drives people crazy. It's the one thing that drives people completely nuts. And it brings out the greed in people. It seems to me you've got a situation in which seven people who don't live at the farm, haven't lived there for years, actually own it.

TF: But they were appointed by someone who had something in mind. Marshall was instrumental, to say the least, in getting that place going, and his wishes should be respected in that they are legitimate.

[Michael Curry arrives and is warmly greeted.]

RM: I'm taping our conversation for my new book, which is a kind of sequel to my first book *Famous Long Ago*.

MC: That's funny. I was driving across the country, and I stopped in Tucson and came across a copy in a giant used bookstore; it looked like an old supermarket.

RM: What year was that?

MC: Just a month ago. There it was, and I grabbed it.

RM: I saw a copy of *Home Comfort* in Paul Krassner's apartment in Venice today, and I was tempted to steal it. The guy's got every counterculture book crammed into his apartment, thousands of them, and piles of used newspapers and magazines in the hallways so you have to walk single file to get past them. So, Michael, what are you up to? You're living here in L.A.?

MC: Yes, I'm teaching geography at UCLA.

RM: Geography? Congratulations. Do you think we're going to get the Big One?

MC: I don't know; are you afraid of it?

RM: Terrified. Anyway, we were talking about Montague, and you are one of the seven people named on the trust. What if any one of those seven decided to be obstreperous? What if someone decided he wants his one-seventh equity out of it?

MC: It's not really that way. It seems to me the way it was set up, we couldn't each get our part out of it.

RM: The way it was written, if any one of the seven should no longer live at the farm, they'd lose their share of the trust.

MC: Right. But then it had these funny provisos, such as if for various reasons they had to spend some time away, then that's really OK. I guess the question is whether fifteen years away is still OK. [Laughter.]

TF: They need a lawyer, no matter what they do. I remember

once under a different set of circumstances at the Wen-
del commune some occupants had to be legally evicted.
People moved in in such a way that it was accepted, but
they turned out to be totally counter to the purpose of
the farm. The people living at Montague are not counter
to the purpose of the farm, but they are very few people, whose principal claim is simply having lived there.
Sam Lovejoy spent some of his time as a lawyer straight-
ening out these kinds of legal situations set up twenty
years ago. The danger is that idealism in itself is not
enough in today's world.

MC: Whatever the disadvantages of the Montague situation, it still exists as a kind of symbol for us. I guess my
problem with the idea of turning it over to a nonprofit
is that I've seen so many nonprofit organizations that
can make it for two or three years but then fail. It's
possible with the way it is now that we can go on until
we die, although I have reservations about just leaving
things go. The danger would be if someone there decided to sue the trust, or if we ever decided to sell,
things could be ticklish. Something needs to be done to
forestall this.

TF: I've learned from the art world that ideals and values are
more or less free-floating. You present a piece of art and
it "floats," but it needs to be supported by its framework. If you literally float it, toss it on the water, it
sinks. There's a relationship there between the support
which is necessary but remains in the background, and
the actuality.

MC: I lived and worked for two-and-a-half years at Shimer
College in Illinois, a traditional college like St. John's
with the Great Books, but in the seventies they started
to run out of money and the trustees decided to close it
down. Certain students and faculty decided to keep it
open, so they took over, sold the campus, and moved it
to Waukegan. At the time there were about thirty students. They decided all faculty would be paid the same
and everything would be run cooperatively and that

students would have an equal say. I moved there, and within six months I because the chief fiscal officer of the college with the assignment of keeping it from folding, with the feds trying to shut it down.

RM: A dramatic story.

TF: And not unrelated to the farm situation.

MC: It turned out to have been not very democratic and not very ideal in any way. There were really three or four people who'd been there a long time, and when new people came in and called them on the fact that it wasn't democratic, that it was being run from the top by these autocrats, they just were nasty until people left and they basically had lasted everybody out. In some ways it's very similar to Montague. What happens is you take on this idea that you embody the ideals of the place, and then anything that's an attack on you is an attack on the ideals of the place and vice versa.

RM: And the person who owns the place is the person who outlasts the others.

TF: We're in another cycle now. Whereas that piece of land could be acquired with a simple signature for twenty-five thousand dollars in 1968, now the university [of Massachusetts, nearby in Amherst] is so growth oriented that land and that place is valuable as a pied-à-terre for the things people want to do. It might be a very good study center for the history of the sixties or contemporary studies. I would hate to see it turn into the private home of a couple of people when it should continue to be what it was. The history of Montague had to do almost entirely with a man who had an incredibly complex personal life. It's not surprising that in his haste to leave the world, [Marshall] left a few loose ends not tied up.

RM: A few little chaotic details.

MC: I just got a long document from Sluggo [Harvey Wasserman] about Marshall. It includes the stuff from the FBI files.

RM: It's by no means certain that he actually committed

suicide. There's just this lingering doubt. In the last
year of his life, Bloom seemed much happier than before. The suspicion is that he may have been hounded to
his death by some threat of exposure of his homosexuality that so humiliated him he preferred to die.

TF: I can believe some of this and more than most people,
but if you want to take a theory like that seriously, you
have to ask what's to be gained by doing this to someone, what are the stakes?

RM: They wanted to shut him down, basically.

TF: If you look at what might have become of Marshall . . .

RM: He could be the editor of the *New York Times*, he had
such great energy.

TF: He cast a long shadow.

MC: I knew all these true believers in the left; they did a lot
of acid, they got into Hare Krishna and a series of
things, and they ended up either being doctrinaire
Marxists or born-again Christians, because that's where
you get the most social support. But it seems the crowd
around Montague and Packer's Corners weren't those
kind of people.

RM: We weren't true believers, Marxists, we didn't belong
to political parties, we didn't even belong to SDS. We
formally rejected an affiliation with SDS because we
were afraid it would make LNS too much of a journalistic arm of a political party. Plus which, speaking for
myself, I was only interested in getting high.

MC: There are easier ways of getting high.

RM: And our leader, Bloom, was a mad genius. The rest of
us were relatively sane, and we've all had to make some
concessions just to stay alive.

～

Missing persons report, continued: **Bill Higgs, Liz
Meisner, Gary Rader, Shirley Clarke,** call home! **Dr.
Steve Brown,** who operated a free clinic for hippies in
Washington, was the forerunner of the HIPpocrates column
in the *Berkeley Barb*. **Warren Sharpe,** *Barb* editor, went on

to edit *San Francisco* and *Focus* magazines. Where are **Kenneth Anger, Stokely Carmichael**? These are our own MIAs, Missing in Activism, Memory in Action.

~

John Wilton is the lanky Australian native who is half of the Mad John and Wonderboy team in *Famous Long Ago*. He came to the U.S. in the 1960s after taking degrees in engineering and became involved with the *AVATAR* underground newspaper in Boston, published by Mel Lyman's notorious Fort Hill community. John's father was the commanding general of the Australian armed forces in Vietnam, one of our few allies in that war, and when John was arrested for selling allegedly pornographic *AVATAR*s in Boston, it made front-page news in Sydney and Melbourne. He later studied the sitar with Indian master Ali Akbar Khan, and he became, along with Sam Lovejoy, one of the No Nukes concert and movement people. He now lives in New York, where he operates the Wilton Hilton at Christopher and Bleecker streets in Greenwich Village.

RM: John, you are one of the seven people named as trustees of the Montague farm, the Fellowship of Religious Youth. What do you think should be done?

JW: Well, I got a letter from Harvey Wasserman about it; he wanted to add about thirty people to the trust. It's a very sticky situation. Nobody seems to know quite what to do, but it's only a matter of time before somebody gets greedy or ruthless. Under the current arrangement, we could never sell it.

RM: You're operating a record company, I've heard. What's it about?

JW: It's Raga Records. We're recording and distributing the music from one artist, Mikhil Banerjee, a very good sitar player, in fact the best. He had more heart than Ravi Shankar. Unfortunately he died, and unfortunately very little of his stuff has been distributed. Indian music in general has lost some of its earlier popularity in this country. There's less interest than there was in the seventies, when I studied at the Ali Akbar Khan School in '72 to '73.

RM: Maybe you can stage a revival.

JW: Could be. I tracked down the original Banerjee recordings from KPFA-FM in Berkeley, and we offer them on cassettes and we hope to offer CDs eventually. It's a small business, but it feels like the right thing to be doing.

RM: Are your ideals realized, John? What's happened in recent years?

JW: You mean as one gets older?

RM: Yes.

JW: Well, I was watching on TV a gay rights demonstration in Washington, D.C., and it was awe-inspiring how heavy it was. The members of ACT UP, they were harassed by the police, harangued by skinheads, the Ku Klux Klan was there, muttering, all this shit was going down. And I would no more take part in something like that nowadays . . . I just couldn't go through it, I couldn't deal with it anymore.

RM: I feel the same way. I stay the hell away from anyplace where there are cops, tear gas. I don't want to get my head bashed in.

JW: And the police just stand by while these guys get bashed.

RM: We should be grateful to them for being out there, although like yourself I wouldn't be there.

JW: And there's a meeting every Monday night, packed with cute boys, but I couldn't even stand to go to a meeting, with all their points of order.

RM: John, we couldn't stand meetings even twenty years ago!

JW: I know. I'm looking forward to going up to my gym to pick up weights. Maybe my workout buddy Fred will be there.

~

Marc Sommer went by the improbable pen name of Gaston

St. Rouet, and we eventually created a town for him: St. Rouet, Arkansas. The last time I found him, in the mid-1970s, he was a Zen monk living in the coastal village of Pescadero, California. **Steve Goldberg** was conceded to be "the most beautiful boy in the world" in *Famous Long Ago*, a Quaker volunteer in Vietnam who joined a Boston radical theater group and was never heard from again. How can these people be simply lost?

~

I. F. Stone was never lost, always on track, so recently died (1989) and so sorely missed. This great muckraker, independent publisher of *I. F. Stone's Weekly*, "Izzy" to us, encouraged us with LNS, gave us research material and backing and political clout, came to our offices once a week with a bag lunch, and taught us a lesson we never forgot: "Don't belong to anyone, even a political group you support and admire. Don't be anybody's mouthpiece. The minute you lose your independence as journalists, you lose your credibility. The country is full of compromised writers and newspapers dependent on advertising. Be a free and brave voice."

~

Marty Jezer is a pacifist who was active in the War Resisters League, Workshop in Nonviolence, and the Resistance antidraft movement when we met in the 1960s. He and I were the original purchasers of the farm at Packer's Corners, although he dropped off the deed because of a federal tax protest, and I later deeded the place to our nonprofit artists' cooperative. More than most, he has remained passionately involved in activist politics and now lives in Montreal with his wife, Mimi, and their child.

MJ: Raymond, what a surprise.
RM: I've been in touch with Verandah, so I know more or less what you're up to. You're in Montreal, right?
MJ: We live in Montreal during the school year, but we still have a house on the farm and as far as I'm concerned, that's home!

RM: Great. It's amazing how long we held on to that place. I was reading *Home Comfort* the other day, and I chuckled over your comment that you loaned your last $2,500 to this absolute madman Raymond Mungo, and he then takes the last hundred dollars of it and buys a car and drives away, leaving you on this abandoned farm. And I said to myself, "Marty was such a saint, giving up the last bucks he had and taking a chance on what could have been a horrible disaster."

MJ: That's all I had. All of us were very brave and very crazy, but it's a good combination.

RM: You wrote several books, didn't you?

MJ: Yes, there was *The Dark Ages*, my book about the 1950s, published by South End Press, and that's in its fifth printing. The printings were not very big, but it sounds impressive. And I wrote a biography of Rachel Carson aimed at the teenaged trade, called *Rachel Carson* and published by Chelsea House. And I'm in a whole bunch of anthologies.

RM: The big news was that you're working on a book about Abbie Hoffman for Rutgers University Press, right?

MJ: Right. How far do you live from L.A.? Because I might fly out there to interview Anita Hoffman, Abbie's first wife.

RM: Just two hours. I'm always going in to Hollywood. You have some competition for books about Abbie, I've heard.

MJ: Yes, Jonah Raskin is working on one and also Johanna Lawrenceson, his third wife.

RM: How did you happen to decide to write a book on him?

MJ: The day I heard Abbie died, I said to myself, "I have to write an article on him," so I called up a magazine in Boston that's an offshoot of South End Press and they said go ahead. I did it, and everyone who read it told me I understood Abbie better than anyone else and should do a book on him. I have an agent, and I got the contract. It has to be finished by August 1990.

RM: How did you and Mimi end up in Montreal?

MJ: Well, she came up here to teach college classes in 1972, and eventually she got tenure. That's why we're kind of stuck up here. Tenure is hard to get and even harder to give up.

RM: Well, she'd be crazy to give it up. Besides, Montreal is one of the best places you could be in Canada.

MJ: We do like it. And my kid is totally fluent in French.

~

Kathleen Kettmann went on from the media wars of the '60s to the consciousness-raising of the '70s, to organizing and running the Great American Peace Walk in the '80s. She worked closely as an aide to Governor Jerry "Moonbeam" Brown of California when he was in office and made the transition to being out of power when he did. As recently as November 1989, she masterminded the successful campaigns that elected the first black governor of Virginia and defeated the ballpark ordinance in postearthquake San Francisco. She is in great demand as a liberal political architect and is one of the bright young hopes for American progressives.

She thinks we can win: we the people, that is, can actually determine our own fate by democratic vote. But she's also battered and beaten down by ferocious opposition. Politics is a nasty game, and as poet and Harvard professor William Alfred said, "We're like skunks, we stink when we're afraid or hurt."

"Kathleen of the laughing eyes" is still in there, slugging it out. "But I don't know how long I can stand it, Ray," she said. "It's a nightmare, but what can I do? I can't stand around and let the bastards get away with murder."

~

Harvey Wasserman, affectionately nicknamed Sluggo in the '60s because of a burly resemblance to the cartoon character, is one of the few original LNS people who is still active in political causes. He has been a leader in the antinuclear power movement since the mid-1970s. His book *Harvey Wasserman's History of the United States* has been in print for more than fifteen years, and he still lectures and writes, while also working for his family's business in Columbus, Ohio.

RM: How has time treated you, Harvey?
HW: Pretty well, I have to say. I have twin daughters, two-and-a-half years old.
RM: The apples of your eye.
HW: Absolutely, although they have kept me up the last couple of nights. It's a great blessing to have kids.
RM: And your books? Is your history book still in print?
HW: Yes, *Harvey Wasserman's History of the United States* has been revised a number of times and is now back in print, published by a small house in New York, Four Walls Eight Windows. They're very progressive, and they did a reasonably nice job with it. My other book, *Killing Our Own*, did very well, had an enormous impact. It was about the health effects of atomic radiation. That's what I continue to do. That's my major calling, my antinuclear work. I've been lecturing on campuses since 1982 and doing a fair amount of op-ed and free-lance writing about nuclear stuff. I had a piece in *Penthouse* in November [1989] on Richard Thornburgh's role in Three Mile Island; he's a nasty guy. And I just got a call from *Library Journal* asking me for a piece on LNS, so I'm glad you called. I took pieces of my [LNS series] "The Adventures of Sluggo" and included that article "Who Stole the Cookie Jar?" that was actually written by the FBI, I don't know if you remember.
RM: I don't recall that particular article, but I have in the book all the stuff from Angus Mackenzie about the FBI's infiltration of the news service. It was all documented in the *Columbia Journalism Review*.
HW: Right.
RM: I'm taking the position that the government tried to

kill us, and we can't say for sure that they *didn't* kill Marshall Bloom. There's enough suspicion that it's something more than mere paranoia.

HW: That's right.

RM: You sent out a letter with suggestions about the LNS farm in Montague. Everybody seems to agree that it can't continue to be owned by seven people who don't live there, that more people should be added to the trust and the place maintained as a trust.

HW: There was a wonderful response to that letter. It was sent to everyone I could think of who was involved with Montague farm, essentially wondering if they might like to join the trust. That farm is very special—it's widely loved and universally viewed as communal property, meant for service, forever in trust, never to be sold. The trick will be to balance the rights of the larger community with the needs of those who choose to live there.

RM: You are one of the people named in the trust, yes?

HW: Right. The important thing is this nuclear stuff. We were very lucky in Montague that the nuke issue came in just as the war was ending, which gave us a tremendous continuity in activism.

RM: What's the situation right now? Are we better or worse off in terms of fighting the nuclear power plants?

HW: I think we've made really great strides. In 1974, when they came in, Nixon was talking about a thousand reactors. There were supposed to be twenty in every state. And basically we've held them to around 120 total. We've won some very big victories. The bottom line is that if there had been no demonstrations at Seabrook, you never would have heard a word about Three Mile Island. We had twenty thousand people at Seabrook nine months before that accident. I'm sure that it played a part in getting the movie *The China Syndrome* made.

RM: Definitely.

HW: There would have been no issue, it wouldn't have

occurred to people, had we not done that. I think we've had every bit as big an impact as the civil rights or antiwar movements. And now the environment is a hot issue. Now we've won another one; it appears we've blocked the nomination of a completely corrupt incompetent to head the nuclear weapons cleanup. We win a few here and there. In Ohio we forced them to convert a nuclear plant to coal. Coal's not the best, but it's certainly safer than nuclear. In Michigan we forced a conversion to natural gas. The map of the U.S. is dotted with nuclear plants that never got built.

RM: Including Seabrook, right? It hasn't gone into operation yet, has it?

HW: No, but we're fighting right now, tooth and nail. We're hanging by our fingernails. At this point they want to open it, and you know this Sununu [former New Hampshire governor and Bush's chief of staff] is a complete nuclear fanatic.

RM: Isn't it Massachusetts that's standing in their way?

HW: Yes, but they've changed the rules now. What they've done now is said, "Evacuation is not an important enough issue to stop the plant." Unfortunately, the courts haven't helped much. The Atomic Energy Commission (AEC) basically gives the industry dictatorial powers, and we haven't been able to crack that in the courts. So we've won politically at the grass roots and economically when we do force a utility to abandon a plant. We almost stopped one near Cleveland; that was one of the karmic twists of my coming back home to Ohio to deal with my family and the family business. All of a sudden I was involved in the fight of my life. I was debating a woman from the utility company at a prep school on the morning the space shuttle blew up. And three days later they had an earthquake at the site, in Ohio if you can believe that. And then Chernobyl happened, and I went on the Phil Donahue show. I did a lot of media in the state as well. I actually wrote a memo to the governor, and he did everything right; he actually rescinded his approval of the evacuation plans, which put him in the same position as Massachusetts, but the Nuclear Regulatory Commission refused to meet with him. Can you believe it? Ohio's the seventh largest state in the country. Then the governor took them to court and lost, so they wound up opening the plant. But we think we've prevented a second unit from being built.

RM: It's good to know you're still in the fight. Most of us haven't changed our ideals, but we've given up being activists.

HW: I was arrested at Diablo Canyon in '84, then again at Seabrook in '89. I interviewed several hundred people over the years who were exposed to radiation, who developed cancer or other radiation-related diseases, or had their children born deformed. Once you've seen that, there's no turning back. Especially now that I have children of my own, it means more than ever. There are four weapons facilities in this state alone. Talk about danger—your farm in Vermont is less than four miles from the Vermont Yankee plant. It was really great sitting there watching the sunset, but who knows what we're breathing, for Christ's sake? Vermont Yankee is a terrible plant. We were right in the gunsights without even really understanding it. In 1980 I got an assignment from *Rolling Stone* to do a story on Three Mile Island a year after the accident, and the stories I heard from local farmers about what happened to their animals were hair-raising, like out of a science fiction movie. I actually saw a dog born with no eyes. Of course, the nuclear plant company said they didn't have anything to do with it. I just don't understand how we can turn away from this.

～

Henry Thoreau has been dead a long time, but he figures consistently as a character in *Famous Long Ago* and his few words here are worth repeating. When he talks in the mascu-

line gender, he and his and so forth, I instinctively translate
into the new language of humankind: she and hers are equal.

> My Friend is not of some other race or family of
> men, but flesh of my flesh, bone of my bone. He is my
> real brother. I see his nature groping yonder so like
> mine. We do not live far apart. . . . As surely as the
> sunset in my latest November shall translate me to the
> ethereal world, and remind me of the ruddy morning of
> youth; as surely as the last strain of music which falls
> on my decaying ear shall make age to be forgotten . . .
> so surely my Friend shall forever be my Friend, and
> reflect a ray of God to me, and time shall foster and
> adorn and consecrate our Friendship, no less than the
> ruins of temples. As I love nature, as I love singing
> birds, and gleaming stubble, and flowing rivers, and
> morning and evening, and summer and winter, I love
> thee, my Friend.

~

Amanda Spake is a writer whose articles have appeared in
many publications and an editor who worked for College
Press Service, *Ms.*, *Mother Jones*, and other liberal media.
For the past three years she has been senior editor of the
Washington Post Magazine, a transition into "Establish-
ment" work. She was one of the featured editors at the 1988
Writers' Jamboree in Carmel.

RM: Amanda, why did you make the move over from liberal
   or radical publications to something like the *Post*?
AS: Why did I make the transition? Well, basically, I had
   always worked with alternative publications and organizations. I guess you could call the College Press Service
   alternative.
RM: I would.
AS: Anyway, these were good learning experiences, but you
   of all people know what it's like, Ray. You have to raise
   the money yourself. It's a seat-of-the-pants operation.

You do it for ideals, not money. Even *Mother Jones* magazine eventually became hierarchical, though, and it wasn't paying salaries or benefits enough to be hierarchical. If you're trading all your time, which is to say your life, you expect to have some power and sense of ownership. I still like freelance writing the best of all, but I decided to try working for the *Post* because I had never worked for a Fortune 500 company, where you don't have to raise the money yourself! And I wanted the credentials and the experience. It was a little bit like "playing the Palace."

RM: So how did you get the job?

AS: Well, every job I've ever gotten was because of my writing. I had done some freelance writing for the *Post*, and the editor said they were starting a new *Washington Post Magazine* with expanded funding and more staff. "Well, you've got editing experience," he said, and I did, with *Ms.* and *Mother Jones* and the *Washington Newsworks*. So I was hired.

RM: Are you a Washington or East Coast native?

AS: Oh, no, I'm from California, and I do miss it terribly. But I couldn't find as good a job out there. I grew up in the suburbs of L.A., in Anaheim, and my dream was always to escape to the big city. Now, after twenty years in big cities, I'm getting kind of tired of them.

RM: Are you working on a book or freelance project in addition to editing?

AS: Yes, I'm pushing ahead on a book about how baby boomers can deal with their aging parents. It's a huge problem, as you know. We're, what, a third of the population, and we've reached the point of having to take care of parents, like suddenly we're the parents and they're the children. My mother died last year, but I had to move her into my apartment after she lost her house. I'd like to go around the country interviewing people about their experiences in this regard. There are some success stories out there, people who are doing well with this problem, but for every one of those, there seem to be several people who are having a horrible time of it.

RM: Yes, I wish I'd read a book about it at the time my father died in 1985. We should have protected his estate better, and now my mom may need care. Good luck with the book. Tell me how you view our experience as activists in the sixties and seventies. Did we create a better nation, or are things worse than ever?

AS: There's no question that our experience as radicals and activists made things better. We changed the course of the Vietnam War, we prevented Nixon from using nuclear weapons in Vietnam, and all of our dissatisfaction with society led to movements like civil rights, the women's movement, and so forth. The general acceptance of the changes we created has made for more openness in American society. I'm sure you saw it in your own family.

RM: I did. I used to think my parents were about the least hip people in America, but one day in the mid-1970s I heard my mother use the word *uptight* and couldn't believe it. That word used to be strictly used by hippies. And even my father, who once believed that marijuana would lead to heroin and just about kill you, finally conceded that it wasn't any worse than beer.

AS: Looking at it historically, we may have sensed that we were the first generation with social spirit, but it's not true. We were part of a great tradition in American history. I believe in certain ideals; I call myself progressive and part of the populist tradition in the U.S. I identify with that very much and will always be progressive. That was accepted while we were growing up, luckily. Earlier generations didn't see the potential. We had a way of viewing things, and it didn't have anything to do with drugs. And the good times are going to come again.

RM: What do you see for us in the future?

AS: In the 1990s we are middle-aged, but I still go to progressive events. In a way it's like our religion, although it's secular, in the same tradition of something like Brook Farm. Our politics define us as a group. The nineties will be a period of trying to reach accommodation with our beliefs while still working to keep our heads above water financially.

Now, when we get elderly, in the twenty-first century, that's when we should have solved major social problems. There will be so many of us that we'll *have* to find housing alternatives, we'll *have* to create health alternatives. The old assumption that your kids will take care of you in your old age just isn't true anymore. Many of us don't even have kids.

My friends and I are talking about buying property together now, while we're earning good money. In the future people may come together in property deals, sort of like an elderly commune.

RM: With everybody having their own private apartment or house?

AS: Yes, I'd think. It's going to be a struggle to deal with money then, but we'll find creative solutions.

~

Good night, brave spirits! These people haven't gone anywhere, but they've retreated from the heroic postures of earlier years into a working framework of living, doing the best job you can do, trying to make a world worth inheriting for our children and a universe we can enjoy today.

Age does tend to wear us down. Sometime after, oh, thirty-five or so, you start feeling aches and pains you never felt before. A slipped disc, pulled muscle, dislocated shoulder, sprained knee, insomnia, indigestion, indignities of all kinds arrive uninvited to the ball, and it's an annoyance to realize that we are no longer young, resilient, and capable of anything.

But we *are* taking care of things. As good boomers, we're caught in the middle, looking after our children and parents both, raising the one and lowering the other six feet under. We have seen the future and its name is "more of the same, but *vive la différence*."

Chapter 12
Soaring into the Millennium

WE BABY BOOMERS, 80 million Americans born between 1946 and 1964, constitute more or less a third of the population. We are the biggest single demographic bulge of a century, and just as we made for a huge youth movement in the 1960s and 1970s, we will create a massive elderly bloc in the early twenty-first century. It will at last be *cool* to be old.

Now there's typical baby boomer thinking for you. Somehow we were always convinced as youngsters that we had invented taste, culture, ethics, the New Age; we were with it, hip, we were *happening*. When middle age and yuppie status symbols came along, they too became de rigeur. Every trend we adopt, every popular song we sing, everything we *do* is being done by a huge mob of people. Our concerns overwhelm the nation.

I like to think that we put an end to the war in Vietnam. Until that war, Americans had almost unanimously supported their government in every previous conflict. But our generation included millions who protested that cruel, imperialist slaughter. Those of us who actually fought in the war bore the worst brunt of its inhumanity. Our Vietnam veterans are still wounded, still in shock.

The battleground of the twenty-first century will not be a foreign field but a crisis in domestic health care. Because the generations following us had many fewer children, we baby boomers will become eligible for social security at a time when the labor force of young and middle-aged people supporting the system is considerably smaller than our own age group. The government assures us that social security will be solvent and reliable for us, but our generation is the first to *stop believing* in the government. Plenty of experts contend that social security will have to be cut back or eliminated altogether, or that it will be eaten up by the national debt. We will have no real security, and we will protest that with our votes and bodies; we will be *real* Gray Panthers.

We aging Americans could adopt a more liberal immigration policy that admits young workers from other countries to live and work here and pay taxes supporting our massive group of groovy oldies. That assumes that the U.S. will continue to be prosperous and thus attractive to immigrants. Or perhaps we can get the government to build communal villages for the boomers, a return to the idealism, sharing, and commonsense economics of Total Loss Farm. We'll listen to rock and roll as "old fashioned" music. Marijuana will be legal for people over sixty.

Basic values will take precedence over fads, and the search for quality will be our Holy Grail in the twenty-first century as we mourn the rise of plastic man and fondly recall the taste of bacon and eggs, foods outlawed by the cholesterol police.

We will dictate fashions nonetheless. Younger people will imitate our favorite clothing, music, video, art, and literature. We are more literate and college-educated than the generations behind us, and we will dominate the popular vote and manage the corporations and cities. In our retirement years we will generate huge new markets for travel, dining, books, culture, entertainment of all sorts. New computers will continually render their predecessors obsolete.

This is it, my mantra. *This is it.* We've been preparing

for it all along, but it kinda snuck up on us. This is the
transition to power that will show us whether we have, in
fact, a better world plan or whether we're just as greedy and
stupid as our forefathers, who raped the earth and polluted
the air, water, and soil for personal wealth. The difference
between us and them is that now the earth is pushed to its
limits. We have to clean up our planet or die.

Euthanasia, the flip side of abortion, will be legalized
in the twenty-first century as an economic move and a comfort for the terminally ill who expressly wish to die. Some
futurists predict that fetal brain tissue will be surgically
transplanted into elderly folks as a remedy for Alzheimer's
disease. Maybe we'll live forever . . .

Oh, come on now. The great storyteller William Saroyan remarked on his deathbed, "I know everybody has to
die sometime, but I always figured I would be the exception." We were raised in a world of exceptions. The war was
over, the economy booming, and the future looked unlim-
ited when television arrived in the early 1950s. We are the
first generation of television, the first to be exposed to mass
marketing of kiddie kulture. We belonged to a group even
then. We wore Davy Crockett coonskin hats, all of us at the
same time. We were members of the Mickey Mouse Club and
regulars at "American Bandstand." *It's got a good beat and I
like to dance to it.* We signed up for the draft, although many
of us later repudiated the war. You gotta believe in magic.

We are today consumed by keeping our families and
jobs, caring for our parents and kids, paying the mortgage.
(If you're lucky enough to have a mortgage; the gap between
homeowners and renters is ever widening, and a frightening
majority of people can't afford to own their home.) But in
the twenty-first century, we'll have time to return to our
ideals and passions, working for a higher good and the
commonweal.

Women hold up half the sky, and women will be the
new leaders of the twenty-first century. They have more
sense than men do anyway, and they tend to live longer.
Women are concerned with nutrition, home, safety, nurtur-

ing, health, and welfare. Wars will end forever.

Depression will haunt us into the twenty-first century and maybe forever. Depression is the biggest killer of all. It got Abbie Hoffman and my father. The media has focused on the high rate of depression in baby boomers, usually arguing that we are disappointed in life because we were promised so much as youngsters. We were disillusioned, this theory goes, when we discovered that we weren't going to get the world on a silver platter, that in fact we can't even do as well as our own parents did and can't retire in the degree of comfort they had.

This explanation may hold true for boomers raised in upper-middle-class homes, but my own upbringing was blue-collar proletarian and we were told to expect a stint in the army and a job in the mills, period. Anything more than that was gravy, and I've feasted on a cosmopolitan life of travel and expression. Depression begone, though it can come and roost on my doorstep these midnights.

Hope is our only cure, and we hope for a world unsullied. Really, what is the point of mankind killing its own, and when will it end? Violence and murder will be replaced by self-mutilation and suicide, aberrations suffered by the unlucky in a world where medical toxins can induce euphoric illusion. Feeling low? Take a pill, feel like a million. Sounds like the '60s again.

No pill will cure our mortality, but we'll leave a world transformed by our generation into a new space, a planet never before visited, an earth beyond hunger and pain. I honestly believe that's possible, that's necessary. If we can break the attachment to personal power and money, we can live together as brothers and sisters under a common sky on common turf and sea. The alternative is unthinkable, although possible. We *could* explode into a million pieces, but somehow we haven't yet.

Hey, we boomers love to have a good time. Who can resist a night on the town, on the planet? Tomorrow we move to the mountains in the high desert of California, far from New York and the important publishing centers, yet in search of the news.

It's tempting to create a rationale for living in the desert—better health, sunshine, exercise, a relaxed community—and these things were all factors in our decision to move. But the truth is simply that we found a house we could afford to buy, with a swimming pool and a Jacuzzi, a double-car garage and panoramic mountain views. The price was nothing, a trifle, a mere breath. The coasts and cities and Midwest plains all rocketed in value, but the desert is still cheap.

And tomorrow we're gone. Our new town has a federal wildlife reserve and Audubon bird sanctuary, public tennis courts and sloping meadows, ballfields of tousle-haired kids. It's got twelve hundred residents at three thousand feet elevation, and nobody locks their doors except when away on vacation. Maybe it'll last, but it's just twenty minutes out of Palm Springs and the developers are coming. Head for the hills!

Go try to buy a house in this country today and you'll find it's not easy, not even for the wealthy. Land fever and greed have arrived simultaneously in the hearts of 250 million people. Anyplace that's desirable and populated has increased in value by extravagant measures in the last decade or so, right? Twenty years ago it was considered an American birthright to have your own home. Young couples bought a place before the baby arrived. Even *ten* years ago anyone with a decent education and some ambition could buy a home. But now it's beyond the reach of most people, most places in the U.S., and that's probably the burning social issue of our times, because it gets you right where you live.

If you don't own your home, if you pay rent, you are paying the upkeep on somebody else's investment. Even after twenty-five or thirty years of living in a rented place you won't own a single nail or board of the structure. We are becoming a nation of landlords and tenants, the few and the many, the rich and the poor, the landed and the thirty-day leaseholds.

OK, the Constitution never promised us a private home for every American citizen, owned in perpetuity for oneself and one's heirs and assigns. Life, liberty, and the pursuit of happiness don't necessarily include homeowners' insurance policies from Allstate. But we boomers have gone nuts for real estate because there's no limit to the number of dollars, francs, or yen in the world—money is infinite—but the number of cubic feet of land on the earth is finite, is absolute, is only so much and no more. Talk about land rushes of history, this is it, this is your last chance to grab an inch. You can't take it with you, but you can live on it now.

This real estate mania is a sad commentary, since it appears there's more than enough empty land to go around. Drive across America and you'll find vistas of empty nature as far as the eye can see. Read *The Solace of Open Spaces* by Gretel Ehrlich. Regard the photos of Ansel Adams. Why are there pockets of unendurable congestion like Calcutta when there are valleys of wide vacancy like Canada?

Because we prefer to gather together. Every map shows hot spots of urban centralization, places where people and marketplace interact. We fill in the blanks. Yesterday's vacant lot is suddenly a 7-Eleven store, the woods beyond Grandpa's farm are now full of tract housing.

And because artificial political divisions have corraled the poor and hungry into national ghettos. El Salvador is a wretched mess, Bangladesh a land mine, Bel Air a millionaire's reserve. Location is everything.

To the desert, then, for the clean air and the coyote's call and a fresh start at forty-three. Thank God we've got modems, fax, telephones, every imaginable electronic device for instant communication, because we *need* to stay in touch. We boomers will network, we will be family. I'll answer every letter, so write.